CHILDREN OF THE HOLOCAUST

Other Books on the Holocaust

Holocaust Memoir Digest Volumes 1 and 2
Compiled and Edited by Esther Goldberg

The Children Accuse
Maria Hochberg-Marianska and Noe Grüss

Six From Leipzig
Gertrude Dubrovsky

Holocaust Literature
Gillian Banner

Salo's Song
Barbara Esser

Have You Seen My Little Sister?
Janina Fischler-Martinho

My Child is Back!
Ursula Pawel

Children of the Holocaust

Editor

Andrea Reiter

VALLENTINE MITCHELL
LONDON • PORTLAND, OR

First published in 2006 in Great Britain by
VALLENTINE MITCHELL
Suite 314 Premier House, 112–114 Station Road,
Edgware, Middlesex HA8 7BJ

and in the United States of America by
VALLENTINE MITCHELL
c/o ISBS, 920 N.E. 58th Street, Suite 300
Portland, Oregon 97213-3786

Website http://www.vmbooks.com

British Library Cataloguing in Publication Data

Children of the Holocaust
1. Jewish children in the Holocaust 2. Holocaust, Jewish (1939–1945), in literature 3. Holocaust, Jewish (1939–1945), in art
I. Reiter, Andrea
940. 5'318'083

ISBN 0 85303 627 6 (paper)

Library of Congress Cataloging-in-Publication Data:

A catalog record has been applied fo

This group of studies first appeared in a special issue of *Holocaust Studies: A Journal of Culture and History*,
Vol.11/2 [ISSN 1359-1371]
published by Vallentine Mitchell & Co. Ltd.

Printed in Great Britain by Antony Rowe Ltd, Chippenham, Wilts

Contents

Kinds of Testimony: Children of the Holocaust

ANDREA REITER

> *Child survivors cannot recollect the Holocaust the way adult survivors do. Their contribution is bound to their experience. But their limited experience is a profound one.*[1]
>
> Aharon Appelfeld.

On Holocaust Memorial Day in January 2004, the University of Southampton hosted a one-day conference on 'Children of the Holocaust' under the auspices of the AHRB Parkes Centre for Jewish/non-Jewish Relations. The eight speakers included well-known academics and doctoral candidates. The topic was approached from a variety of angles and the papers covered issues of different ethnic groups (Jews, Sinti and Romany) and art forms (texts and pictures), as well as distinct groups among the persecuted and the saved (for example, the *Kindertransport* children). The participants of about 40 academics, students, teachers and the interested public thus received a rich picture, which generated lively discussions well into the lunch and tea breaks.

Our guest of honour was Thomas Geve, who at the age of 15 was liberated from Buchenwald. Geve had also survived Auschwitz and Groß-Rosen, though his mother perished in Auschwitz. In 1946 he joined his father, who had escaped to Britain in 1939. Geve trained as an engineer and in 1950, at the age of only 20, he moved to Israel where he lives today.[2]

Immediately after liberation, while he was regaining strength in Buchenwald between April and June 1945 before his departure from the camp, the young Geve started to record his memory of the camps in a series of small pencil drawings. With the encouragement of fellow inmates and his carers, he produced 79 drawings.[3] By courtesy of the Gedenkstätte Buchenwald, a selection of 42 of these drawings were brought to Southampton. An exhibition of them, opened by

Geve, complemented the academic sessions of the conference. The artist's comments on his work made the experience on which it was based more tangible for the viewers. Participants were also able to view the film *Nothing but Life* (dir. Wilhelm Rösing, 1997), which captures Geve reminiscing about his camp experience in Buchenwald. The drawings and the film, together with the presence of Thomas Geve, added a sense of immediacy to the conference, which made it so memorable for all participants.

* * *

Increasing temporal distance from the Nazi concentration camps – recently, the sixtieth anniversary of the liberation of Auschwitz was commemorated – has had an impact on the artefacts associated with the Nazi atrocities. At least three effects can be identified. First, the Holocaust has been taken up by authors who were not themselves affected by the events, such as in Martin Amis' *Time's Arrow* (1991), Bernhard Schlink's *The Reader* (1995), Anne Michaels' *Fugitive Pieces* (1996), or W.G. Sebald's *Austerlitz* (2001). Secondly, survivors who, for one reason or another, have hitherto chosen to remain silent have begun to speak out. These survivors, now in their late seventies, were mere children during their incarceration. Hence they have not only to contend with the considerable time that has elapsed between their experience and their report about it, but their camp experiences themselves were of a different kind from that of the grown-ups. Nevertheless, among those testimonies are arguably two of the genre's most interesting examples: Ruth Klüger's *Weiter leben: Eine Jugend*[4] and Imre Kertész's *Roman eines Schicksallosen*.[5]

The distance from the event is also responsible for a third phenomenon, which could be termed the disposability of the Holocaust as a metaphor. In public discourse this became most apparent during the Balkan Wars of the 1990s. In literary discourse it gained certain notoriety with the so-called Wilkomirski affair. *Bruchstücke: Aus einer Kindheit 1939–1948* was published in 1995 as the memoir of the self-claimed Jewish child survivor Binjamin Wilkomirski, but was discovered two years later to be a fraud.[6] Apart from the potential damage this affair has inflicted on the artistic representation of the Holocaust, it opened up the general discussion about the authenticity and textuality of camp testimonies. Elsewhere, I have argued that these questions do not necessarily support the views of those conservative historians who, in the name of ethics, have demanded restraint of the artistic licence.[7] On the contrary, the narrative devices that 'Wilkomirski' adopted and that had persuaded even the experts to read the text as an authentic memoir have demonstrated that any text about the Holocaust, whoever wrote it and with whatever intention, can only mediate the facts.[8] And this insight, while the historian may deplore it and devise strategies to minimise it, nevertheless points at the essence of literature.

In 1998 the University of Marburg in Germany hosted an international and interdisciplinary conference on the representation of children of the Holocaust. This was not only one of the first major academic events on German soil devoted to Holocaust literature but its theme and programmatic title – *'Für ein Kind war das anders'* (Things were different for a child) – hinted at the ambition of the organisers to open up a new academic discourse about the representation of the Holocaust.[9] Thus all contributions dwelt either on the idiosyncrasy of the child's perception of traumatic events or on the strategies the adult authors developed to represent this idiosyncrasy. Not all Holocaust testimonies featuring children in camps are retrospective, of course. There are some diaries, the most widely known being that of Anne Frank. There is Charlotte Salomon's pictorial autobiography *Leben? oder Theater?*, comprising 769 plates, which she composed between 1940 and 1942 during her exile in France.[10] In his forthcoming book Nicholas Stargardt discusses an exceptional body of children's drawings, from Theresienstadt. These works, like the diaries Sue Vice discusses in this volume, are artefacts contemporaneous with persecution. Geve's drawings occupy a midway position between the records of persecution documented in camp and those produced retrospectively during the first years after liberation. A number of these children who survived the persecution later produced a second book on their experiences. These new texts, often produced in direct response to the reception of their first book, offer corrections or modifications in order to re-evaluate memories of their experiences from a greater distance, while also taking account of the changed public discourse about the Holocaust and its victims.[11]

So what is it that distinguishes the diaries and reports by children from those of adults? First and foremost, it is the child's limited perspective based on its world view, still very much in flux and more impressionable. The child's interpretation of its perceptions is less guided by logic than by the magical world of the fairy tale. Barbara

Bauer has shown how, and to what extent, *l'universe concentrationnaire* caused a disorientation of the children who failed to understand that the rules they had internalised during their short lives prior to the camps did not apply in a world turned upside down. Bauer likens the children's conduct in the camps to the irrational behaviour of Don Quixote.[12] However, while the out-of-place actions of this tragic knight are designed to amuse the reader, such inappropriate behaviour by the children in camp as the playful identification with their persecutors breaks a moral taboo. Moreover, children are less guided by self-censorship. Mindful of this, the editors of children's diaries such as Anne Frank's tried to purge potentially controversial sections of the text prior to its publication.[13]

Adult authors who try to emulate the child's experience by recreating the limited perspective of the child's gaze resort to a literary device. The reader perceives this as an even greater taboo and reacts with shock.[14] The contravention of beliefs and values concerning survival, hitherto regarded as sacrosanct, seem to be a hallmark of more recent camp memoirs. Until the late 1980s mothers of camp survivors, for example, were above criticism. This is probably due to the fact that, as research has shown, a mother was instrumental in helping her (female) child survive.[15] Even Cordelia Edvardson could not bring herself in *Gebranntes Kind sucht das Feuer*, first published in 1984,[16] to say anything critical about her mother, the German novelist Elisabeth Langgässer, who did not accompany her to the camp. Only five years later, in her second book *Die Welt zusammenfügen*,[17] does she have the courage to deplore her mother's domineering presence, which still haunts her in her dreams. Ruth Klüger may have faced a similar situation, but abandoned a report she attempted to write soon after her release because it omitted her complicated relationship with her mother.[18] Apart from the effort to represent their struggle for survival more truthfully, the violation of erstwhile taboos, as much as the child's perspective, represents a conscious effort of the survivors to defamiliarise the life in the camps for the reader. By the 1990s the Holocaust had been iconicised in and by the public domain to an extent, threatening to make it 'invisible'. Auschwitz and Buchenwald were increasingly detached from the historical circumstances to serve as metaphors for genocide, the Holocaust made an example of trauma. The child's perspective, as a means to force the reader to consider the Holocaust anew, was also a reaction to the perceived saturation of post-war society with images of the camps. While newsreels featuring heaps of shoes and other artefacts shown immediately after liberation were designed to shock the viewer, over the years these images increasingly lost their effect as metonymic expressions of suffering.

Apart from the effect of the child's perspective on the reception of testimonies, in aesthetic terms it increased the literarisation of discourse about the Holocaust. The stylistic and narrative devices approximated these texts to Holocaust fiction. Poetic structure and limited perspective, as found in the novels by Ilse Aichinger, Anna Gmeyner and Martin Amis, are also features in the more recent texts of survivors. This leads to the obvious question: does this make the survivor texts less authentic than earlier testimonies, where the foregrounding of (all) literary characteristics is explicitly avoided? It is true that childhood memory is considered to be less reliable than adult memory, not only because of the time that separates the adult looking back at his or her childhood self, but also as much due to the child's original perception.[19] But it is not the unearthing of new facts that we should expect from these more recent texts about the camps: it is rather our comprehension of the individual's experience that has been enhanced. The sociologist Gabriele Rosenthal, who has worked with several generations of survivors, insists that what is important for her analysis of the narrative interviews she conducts is the way survivors (and their descendents) remember certain incidents, rather than that they are remembered accurately.[20]

The Israeli novelist Aharon Appelfeld, who survived internment and concentration camps as a small child, insists on the validity of the representation of the child survivor by the adult. Children's 'recollections are tiny and when they come to recall what happened to them during the war they mobilise fantasy, sensation and feelings to reconstruct the past'.[21] Appelfeld does not claim that these testimonies can be factual. But this makes them no less valid. Indeed, their reconstructedness turns them into literature: 'No wonder that from them began the Holocaust literature'. Because children had no memory of their life prior to camp, nor had they constructed a frame of reference against which they could measure their camp experience, and as adult writers they are not able to concentrate on surface data and experience. The former child victims thus resort to imagination to recreate the atmosphere and emotions that, according to Freud, cannot be part of memory.

In chapter three of their book *Textual Memory*, entitled 'Memory's Realism', Peter Middleton and Tim Woods draw on Lacan's appropriation of Freud's concept of *Nachträglichkeit* for post-structuralist theory.[22] This concept, which has to do with the resurfacing of trauma that had been repressed, seems particularly pertinent for the conceptualisation of childhood Holocaust experience, in almost a literal sense. The child victims tried to put the trauma of an early experience of persecution and threat of death to one side in order to cope with life after survival. While this is also true for adult survivors,[23] children, unlike the adults, still continued to construct their fundamental identities after release. A memorable example of how these identities inform their later testimonies is Ruth Klüger's feminist approach to camp experience. By the time the child survivors were ready to confront their early memories these had to be squared with their increased knowledge of the historical events. 'When the people who were adults during the war came to tell their story, their emphasis was on the chronicle; names, places, dates', Appelfeld observed. For children facts and data were of little relevance: 'For them the Holocaust was life, the only life they knew'.[24] As this combines taboo violation with potential unreliability, it comes as little surprise that the reception has reacted with considerable reservation to any subsequent transformation of Holocaust memory into text. Not only Appelfeld has had to experience this.[25]

* * *

All but two of the essays assembled in this volume were presented as papers at the Southampton conference. With her essay 'Children's Voices and Viewpoints in Holocaust Literature', Sue Vice gives a succinct analysis of contemporary and retrospective texts by children and about children. She can show how, especially in retrospective texts, the adult's presentation of the child's viewpoint overlays its voice. In diaries, it is the process of editing which obscures the child's language. While in this case it is only with knowledge extraneous to literature that we can say with confidence that the child's voice is not genuine, we might expect immediacy to the child at least in the rare instance where a child's text is published unedited. But even in this case, Vice argues, there is always the reader's hindsight and additional knowledge which interferes. Therefore it is not surprising that she comes to the rather pessimistic conclusion that none of the texts that she has analysed is actually capable of relaying the authentic voice of the child; indeed, impossible ever to convey.

While this is plausible for a text the situation may be different when it comes to the pictorial testimony. In 'Drawing the Holocaust in 1945', Nicholas Stargardt focused on the pictures drawn by two boys who survived the camps and later were encouraged to record their memories in a set of pencil drawings. Stargardt's contribution dwells on the genesis and rationale of Thomas Geve's work to which I have already referred. He also shows how Geve's drawings served as a model for similar artwork produced by a group of surviving Jewish children who, like Kalman Landau, had been taken to a Swiss home after liberation. He also looks at features generic to children's depictions of life in camp, such as exaggerated perspective.

Susan Tebbutt discusses another artist of the Holocaust in her contribution on 'Stolen Childhood: Austrian Romany Ceija Stojka and her Past'. Stojka and her family were imprisoned in Bergen-Belsen camp as 'Gypsies'. In contrast to Geve she first recorded her experience of persecution in literary form in 1988; but it was not until a decade and a half later that she started publishing her pictorial art. As a Romany, Stojka suffered marginalisation even after she was liberated. Both in post-war Germany and in Austria, 'Gypsies' were not regarded as Holocaust victims and, until quite recently, had no claim to compensation. What is more, the public's contempt for this minority was not really shaken until the murder of four Romanies in the most eastern of Austria's provinces, the Burgenland, in 1995.[26] Given this situation it is therefore of little surprise that Stojka's Holocaust art not only records past persecution but also documents her attempt at self-ascertainment *in lieu* of her whole people. This becomes especially graphic in the colourful depictions of aspects of Romany life.

The following two essays are about distinct groups of survivors: that of the so-called *Kindertransport* children and that of the '*Mischlinge*', or children of religiously mixed parentage. In her essay 'Between Adult Narrator and Narrated Child: Autobiographical Writing by Former Members of the *Kindertransporte*', Andrea Hammel considers these texts as examples of the interface between self-narration and historical resource. This is expressed in the tension between group identity, reinforced by the 'reunion' of former *Kindertransport* children in London in 1989, and individual recollections of the struggle to acquire a new language and adapt to a strange way of life, all under the duress that the loss of the biological family caused.

While the experience and the memories shared by the former *Kindertransport* children give them an identity from which they can draw strength, members of the other distinct group discussed here were compelled to survive the Nazi regime as individuals. Even after its end, as Cathy Gelbin demonstrates in her essay 'Between Persecution and Complicity: The Life Story of a Former "Jewish *Mischling*"', this group of victims found it difficult to know where their allegiance lay. Though they were neither Jewish nor 'Aryan' according to Nazi race laws, their survival originally hinged on the protection of the 'Aryan' parent and later, when even *Mischlinge* were subject to transports to the camps, on avoiding detection. In her analysis of an interview with one *Mischling*, Gelbin shows how this status led to a disturbed identity formation in the young man and even to eventual identification with the persecutor. For this reason, this group of survivors found it difficult after 1945 to talk about their past experiences. Gelbin's interviewee seems to have rebuilt his life at the expense of emotional engagement. During the war this disposition allowed him to disregard Jewish suffering and thereafter to dispel self-reproach.

The connection between victimhood and identity is also the issue of the two essays which conclude this volume. In '"I wish I could be allowed to choose who I am": Jurek Becker, Victim Identity and Identity Crisis in Post-War Germany', Catherine Piggott traces the emergence of Becker's Jewish identity in one of his essays and in a short story. She demonstrates how this writer only gradually accepted that his Jewishness lay in his lost ancestral background, which was preserved in family narratives that used to be told time and again. Cut off from this tradition by the *Shoah*, the only way for him to carry on this tradition is to promulgate the story by writing it down.

Jurek Becker was only eight years old when he was liberated from Sachsenhausen. Less than ten years separate him from the children born to Holocaust survivors after the war. It is therefore not surprising that his search for identity is, as Piggott points out, not wholly dissimilar from that faced by the so-called second generation. In recent years, not only psychologists but also novelists have begun to take an interest in the effect of the Holocaust on the children of survivors. In her essay 'Inheriting the Holocaust: Transfer of Trauma in Doron Rabinovici's *Suche nach M.*', Denise Dick applies to this fictional text by a young Austrian Jewish writer the theory of trans-generational transfer of trauma that had been developed for the analysis of empirical data by Dan Bar-On and Gabriele Rosenthal. She examines how the parents' unresolved past of persecution impacts on the children who are obsessed either with identifying the guilt in their compatriots, or in a surreal act of over-identification take this guilt upon themselves. Either option continues the parents' unwillingness to confront the past and therefore cannot lead to a positive self-identity or to a successful socialisation of the individual.

NOTES

I offer my thanks to Dr Steve Taverner for administrative help with organising the conference. Without his energetic support this event could not have happened. I am also grateful to Professor David Cesarani and the AHRB Parkes Centre for the generous financial support, to Frau Ursula Härtl from the Gedenkstätte Buchenwald for sending the exhibition of Thomas Geve's drawings, and to Stephen Foster from the John Hansard Gallery at the University of Southampton for arranging for the pictures to be exhibited.

1. Aharon Appelfeld, 'A Different Testimony', in Walter Schmitz (ed.), *Erinnerte Shoah: Die Literatur der Überlebenden* [The Shoah Remembered: Literature of the Survivors] (Dresden: Thelem, 2003), pp.3–7 (here p.7).
2. See Thomas Geve, *Es gibt hier keine Kinder – Auschwitz, Groâ-Rosen, Buchenwald: Zeichnungen eines kindlichen Historikers* [There are not Children Here – Auschwitz, Groâ-Rosen, Buchenwald: Drawings of a Child Historian] (Wallstein: Göttingen, 1997), p.9.
3. Ibid., p.10.
4. Ruth Klüger, *Weiter leben: Eine Jugend* (Göttingen: Wallstein, 1992); published in English under the title *Still Alive: A Holocaust Girlhood Remembered*, with a foreword by Lore Segal (New York: The Feminist Press, 2001).
5. Imre Kertész, *Roman eines Schicksallosen* (Berlin: Rowohlt, 1996). This book first appeared in Hungarian under the title *Sorstalanság* in 1975, but only in its German translation did it start to be noticed by a wider public and in 2002 earned Kertész the Nobel Prize for Literature. An English version of the book is entitled *Fateless* (Evanston, IL: Northwestern University Press, 1992).
6. Binjamin Wilkomirski, *Bruchstücke: Aus einer Kindheit 1939–1948* (Frankfurt am Main: Suhrkamp, 1995); in English, *Fragments: Memories of a Childhood 1939–1948*, trans. Carol Brown Janeway (New York: Schocken, 1996). On a documentation of the affair, see Stefan Mächler, *Der Fall Wilkomirski: Über die Wahrheit einer Biographie* (Zürich: Pendo, 2000); and Irene Dieckmann and Julius H. Schoeps (eds.), *Das Wilkomirski-Syndrom: Eingebildete Erinnerungen oder von der Sehnsucht, Opfer zu sein* (Zürich: Pendo, 2002); Andrea Reiter, 'Memory and Authenticity: The Case of Binjamin Wilkomirski', in Peter Gray and Kendrick Oliver (eds.), *The Memory of Catastrophe* (Manchester and New York: Manchester University Press, 2004), pp.132–45.
7. See Andrea Reiter, 'Authentischer Bericht oder Roman: Einige Überlegungen zur Typologie von Holocaust-Texten', in Anne Betten and Konstanze Fliedl (eds.), *Judentum und Antisemitismus: Studien zur Literatur und Germanistik in Österreich* (Berlin: Schmidt, 2003), pp.120–31.
8. See Barbara Bauer and Waltraud Strickhausen, 'Erklärung zum Fall "Binjamin Wilkomirski": Ein Epilog', in Barbara Bauer and Waltraud Strickhausen (eds.), *'Für ein Kind war das anders': Traumatische Erfahrungen jüdischer Kinder und Jugendlicher im nationalsozialistischen Deutschland* (Berlin: Metropol, 1999), pp.54–63.
9. For the published proceedings of this conference, see ibid.

10. *Charlotte: Life or Theatre? An Autobiographical Play: Charlotte Salomon*, with an introduction by Judith Herzberg, trans. Leila Vennewitz (London: Allen Lane, in association with Gary Schwartz, 1981). See also Sabine Dahmen, 'Charlotte Salomons Darstellung ihrer Kindheit und Jugend in Berlin', in Bauer and Strickhausen (eds.), *'Für ein Kind war das anders'*, pp.340–63.
11. See, for example, Elie Wiesel, *Tous les fleuves vont à la mer* (Paris: Seuil, 1994); Colin Davis, 'Reviewing Memory: Wiesel, Testimony and Self-Reading', in Helmut Peitsch *et al.* (eds.), *European Memories of the Second World War* (Oxford: Berghahn, 1999), pp.122–30; Kitty Hart, *Return to Auschwitz: The Remarkable Life of a Girl who Survived the Holocaust* (New York: Athenäum, 1985); Andrea Reiter, 'Die autobiographischen Berichte ehemaliger Konzentrationslagerhäftlinge im Englischen Exil: Bruno Heilig, Ella Lingens, Kitty Hart', *Zeitgeschichte*, Erika Weinzierl (ed.), Vol.19, Nos.5–6 (1992), pp.172–86. Thomas Geve, *Youth in Chains* (Jerusalem: Mass, 1958), was a written testimony for which his drawings served as *aide mémoire*; 42 years later he produced *Aufbrüche: Weiterleben nach Auschwitz* (Konstanz: Südverlag, 2000); Andreas Disselnkötter, 'Nachträglichkeit des Schreibens in der "Post-Holocaust Ära"', in Schmitz (ed.), *Erinnerte Shoah*, pp.42–60.
12. Barbara Bauer, 'Die Immoralität der Nazi-Welt aus der Sicht von Kindern und Jugendlichen', in Bauer and Strickhausen (eds.), *'Für ein Kind war das anders'*, pp.230–55.
13. See, for example, Carol Ann Lee, *Roses from the Earth: The Biography of Anne Frank* (London: Viking, 1999), 'Afterword', pp.256–9, 281.
14. For this and the following, see Andrea Reiter, 'Die Funktion der Kinderperspektive in der Darstellung des Holocaust', in Bauer and Strickhausen (eds.), *'Für ein Kind war das anders'*, pp.215–30.
15. See, for example, Hans Keilson, *Sequential Traumatization in Children: A Clinical and Statistical Follow-up Study on the Fate of the Jewish War Orphans in the Netherlands* (Jerusalem: Magnes Press, 1992).
16. Cordelia Edvardson, *Gebranntes Kind sucht das Feuer* (Swedish original 1984; Munich: Hanser, 1986).
17. Cordelia Edvardson, *Die Welt zusammenfügen* (Munich: Hanser, 1989).
18. Ruth Klüger, 'Literatur als konstruktive Provokation' (interview with Brigitte Feichtner), *SALZ 71* (April 1993), pp.10–12.
19. See Margaretta Jolly (ed.), *Encyclopaedia of Life Writing*, 2 vols. (London and Chicago: Fitzroy Dearborn Publishers, 2001).
20. See, for example, Gabriele Rosenthal, 'Erzählte Lebensgeschichte zwischen Fiktion und Wirklichkeit: Zum Phänomen "falscher" Identitäten', in Dieckmann and Schoeps (eds.), *Das Wilkomirski-Syndrom*, pp.216–35. For a discussion of the false memory debate of the 1990s in the US, see Aleida Assmann, *Erinnerungsräume: Formen und Wandlungen des kulturellen Gedächtnisses* (Munich: Beck, 1999), pp.266–72. Assmann, however, also insists on the truth in false memory due to the apodictic quality of affective memory which is incorrigible, ibid., p.274.
21. In Schmitz (ed.), *Erinnerte Shoah*, p.6.
22. Sigmund Freud, *Standard Edition of the Complete Psychological Works of Sigmund Freud*, 24 vols., trans. and ed. James Strachey with Anna Freud, assisted by Alic Strachez and Alan Tyson (London: Hogarth Press and the Institute for Psychoanalysis, 1953–73), vol.11, p.181; quoted in Peter Middleton and Tim Woods, *Textual Memory* (Manchester: Manchester University Press, 2000), p.101.
23. See, for example, Jorge Semprun, *Literature or Life?* (New York: Viking, 1997).
24. In Schmitz (ed.), *Erinnerte Shoah*, pp.5, 6.
25. See Disselnkötter, 'Nachträglichkeit des Schreibens in der "Post-Holocaust Ära"', pp.42–60.
26. See, for example, Monika Fischer, 'To be or not to be', http://www.univie.ac.at/Very-Vienna/magazin/artikel/11/elf.html, accessed 18 February 2005.

Children's Voices and Viewpoints in Holocaust Literature

SUE VICE

Voice Versus Viewpoint

I began thinking about the area of children's-eye views of the Holocaust in response to Binjamin Wilkomirski's *Fragments*. As is now well known, this was published as the memoir of a child of the camps, then shown to be fiction.[1] The controversy made me wonder, first, how many other works there are about children's experiences during the Holocaust years; and whether the striking techniques used in *Fragments*, of disrupted chronology and artfully simple language, were used in these authentic works too. In this essay, I will approach children's-eye-view works specifically *as texts*, considering above all their narrative construction.[2] Such an approach can preserve what is distinctive about the experience of children during the Holocaust years, and acknowledge the terrible loss of one million children during that time, without falling prey to what Norman Geras calls 'morbid pieties',[3] which the subject might seem to encourage.

Clearly the features of voice and viewpoint mentioned in the title of this essay are quite different. Representing a child's voice means that his or her own language would have to be present in a text. On the other hand, representing a child's viewpoint usually means that an adult narrator describes how events seemed to his or her younger self. As the critic Shlomith Rimmon-Kenan puts it, 'speaking and seeing, narration and focalization' are often separate in literary works,[4] even when they seem to originate in the same first-person utterance; typically, in children's Holocaust texts the person who sees or focalises events is the child, while the one who speaks about or narrates them is the adult.

I will begin with two examples in which it may appear that the child's own discourse is present within the adult's narration. I will then analyse further instances from different genres of Holocaust writing, ranging from testimony to fiction, to see whether or not the child's own voice is ever locatable. The first is an episode from *Memory Fields*, Shlomo Breznitz's memoir of living in hiding in a convent orphanage in Bratislava during the war. It shows clearly that while the reader may gain the illusion of the presence of a child's voice, what we read is, rather, a combination of the adult narrator's voice and the focalisation or viewpoint of the child. In this episode, the commander of the local German garrison visits the orphanage at Christmas; Shlomo and his sister Judith are the only children who know the words to the carol 'Silent Night' in German. As they sing, however, Shlomo realises that the children are giving themselves away by their very success:

> In a flash I finally understood: Why was it that the two of us were the only ones to know the German version of this song? Where were the rest? There were no others because in this country only Jews (*Jews*) understood German. The person above the medals must have known this, too; after all, it was he who had trapped us.[5]

Despite appearances, there is no trace here of a child's language. The boy's perceptions are paraphrased by the adult, as is clear in the verb tenses: the phrase, he 'must have known this, too', is a retrospective deduction. The repeated, italicised version of the word 'Jews' in parentheses is an approximation by the adult narrator of the child's sudden realisation that the danger of being recognised was a reality. We do not even read the individual words that the child used. Calling the commander 'the person' is a nod at a child's ignorance of terminology and rank, but this word appears within a sentence fully informed by hindsight. What does remain instead is a literal instance of a child's perspective, in the phrase 'the person above the medals': we see the commander from below as the child looks up past his uniform to his face.

A slightly different example is from Louis Begley's autobiographical novel *Wartime Lies*. There is no direct speech at all in this first-person novel, and the characters' voices are blended into the narrator's in a sustained example of free indirect discourse. This is true even of the voice of Maciek, the little boy – and the narrator's younger self – who is hiding with his aunt in Warsaw by masquerading as a gentile. For instance, we read what appears to be the boy's own voice describing his preparations for communion:

> I also found, as I studied the book [of prayers] and listened to Father P., that my personal situation was desperate and despicable. There was no salvation except through grace, and grace could be acquired only through baptism … I asked Father P. whether savages living in our time away from the church could be saved if they were good, and he was very clear about it: the ministry of Jesus was complete. Virtue without grace could not suffice.[6]

However, as the past tense indicates, this is the voice of the adult narrator. In particular, the phrase 'desperate and despicable' shows this, with its arch alliteration and dark humour. Parts of the extract may still seem to be the reproduction of a child's voice, even if a fictional one. The child is clearly repeating Father P.'s words when he says, 'There was no salvation except through grace', and 'virtue without grace could not suffice'. Some childlike vocabulary is used, such as the word 'savages', and the phrase 'if they were good'. But in fact, as these words are not directly cited – there are no quotation marks – they are not a transcription of a child's voice. Instead, they consist of a mingled utterance, partly the child's and partly the adult narrator's voice as well.

Diaries

As we can see, it is hard to find examples of texts in which a child's voice – as distinct from viewpoint – is heard unmediated, on its own terms and without the interference or additions of an adult, and of adult hindsight. The reader might think that such a voice, even if absent from memoirs such as Breznitz's and survivor fiction such as Begley's, would be perceived in texts written by children at the time of the events themselves. The following are some instances from Holocaust diaries written by children and teenagers. The first is from Mary Berg's *Warsaw Ghetto: A Diary*, which was published in the US as early as 1944 when Berg was 20. Berg's family were able to leave the Warsaw Ghetto in 1943, due to her mother's American nationality, in exchange for prisoners of war. Her diary entry for 26 June 1941 begins, 'I am writing this in the bomb shelter of our house.

I am on night duty, as a member of the home air defense'; and it ends, 'I think there is an alarm now; yes, a long blast of the siren. I must run to awaken the commandant'.[7] Berg even picks up her pen on the train that takes her family from Warsaw in 1943: 'A few minutes ago I woke from my sleep ... Our train is moving in the direction of Poznan, not Oswiecim'.[8] It appears that there is an extremely close fit here between the 'I' who writes these entries, and the 'I' who is their subject. It is as if we are reading Berg's own voice as it speaks in the midst of events. However, it turns out that this impression of contemporaneity is staged. Berg's diary was rewritten and edited for publication soon after her arrival in New York, and we might wonder if she went out of her way to emphasise moments which seemed particularly authentic – that is, which emphasised the very moment of writing. In fact, this text is a hybrid of diary and memoir, affected by the very hindsight usually missing from diaries.

Mary Berg survived the Holocaust to edit her diary, but even the death of the child-diarist during the war cannot guarantee that the voice we read is authentic, or that retrospection has not crept in. Thirteen-year-old Éva Heyman wrote a diary during her internment in the Budapest Ghetto; the diary ends before her deportation to Auschwitz in 1944, where she died. The diary was in the hands of her mother and stepfather for several years after the war, leading critics to ask whether everything we read is Éva's own words.[9] Once we begin to question this, the diary's irony – arising from a clash between Éva's youthful frame of reference and the adult reality she experiences – appears overly self-conscious for such a young writer, for instance in Éva's description of life in the 'ghetto-camp':

> The most awful thing of all is that the punishment for everything is death. There is no difference between things; no standing in the corner, no spankings, no taking away food, no writing down the declension of irregular verbs one hundred times the way it used to be in school. Not at all: the lightest and heaviest punishment – death.[10]

We may be disappointed to think that this is not all Éva Heyman's own voice. But I would argue that the multi-voiced and temporally complex nature of apparently simple diaries is a positive thing. Even in cases like the Lódz Ghetto diary of an anonymous boy, or Anne Frank's diary, where the authenticity of the diarist's own words is not in question, there is a double-voiced element of a different, historical kind.

The next example is from the anonymous diary written in the Lódz Ghetto in Poland, by a boy who wrote during a few months in 1944. The diary is known as '*Les Vrais Riches*' because, due to the scarcity of paper, the boy wrote on the pages of François Coppée's nineteenth-century French novel of that title. The anonymous boy sees his diary as the means of recording – and even hastening – the passing of time, which, as he notes, in itself might save lives: 'When I write these lines, I don't know for sure if the outsettling [deportation] has been wholly stopped – or partly only, but it is after all good news, because time plays a considerable part at present'.[11] He starts another entry, 'Actually I have nothing to diarize':[12] here, the act of writing itself marks the crucial passage of time, rather than constituting a record of particular events. In the case of '*Les Vrais Riches*' diary it seems that if enough days can pass, then the Nazis will, literally, run out of time. This was a reasonable thought on the boy's part at the time, as the Red Army reached the River Vistula near Lódz on 1 August 1944; but the reader, with hindsight, knows that the Russians did not liberate the city until January 1945, and the boy is thought to have perished before this date. The child's voice is not unitary, but is overlaid or even answered by the reader's retrospective knowledge.

A further example of a child's voice which is crucially altered by the reader's historical knowledge is that of Yitskhok Rudashevski in his *Diary of the Vilna Ghetto*. Rudashevski writes in September 1942, when he is 15: 'It is dusk. "We have staved off another day", the women say to each other'.[13] This notion of 'staving off' is also clear in the next quotation, as if Rudashevski's diary were not just about, but actually facilitating, the passage of time itself:

> My determination to study [and thus to write] has developed into something like defiance of the present which hates to study, loves to work, to drudge. No, I decided. I shall live with tomorrow, not with today.[14]

This commentary on diurnal composition suggests a new relation between the writer and time in a child's Holocaust diary. The passage of time is not just recorded, but – as if this were a new kind of relativity – the diarist implies that the act of daily record itself may have an effect on the speed at which time passes. That is, the diary does not just record the child's voice itself, but acts as a temporal measuring device at an over-determined historical moment. Once more, a complex notion of viewpoint takes over from the simpler one of voice.

In the case of Anne Frank's diary, it is again the reader in the present who adds an extra dimension to her voice. In several entries from Frank's diary, we can see an intersection between adolescent concerns and concerns about living in hiding. Frank's frequent wish for adulthood and self-determination is barely distinguishable from fears about the war and hopes for its end in these examples:

> Now I think either about unhappy things or about myself.
>
> Oh, what kind of bombshell is about to burst now? If only I weren't so involved in all these skirmishes! If only I could leave here!
>
> I'm longing – really longing – for everything: conversation, freedom, friends, being alone.[15]

Frank does not separate the 'unhappiness' and 'skirmishes' of family life from those of life in hiding in occupied Amsterdam. The reader, however, cannot help but read her wish to 'leave' or 'be alone' as an unwitting reference to both. In other words, even in these cases of diaries where the child or teenager records external events, the act of writing itself transforms his or her voice into a comment on keeping a diary at all in such circumstances, and what it was like to live in the midst of momentous events. We do not read these diaries primarily as historical documents, or as authentic records of the child's subjectivity, but rather as narratives which exhibit historical or even tragic irony.

Testimony and Memoir

The next category in which we might expect to find the voice of a child is that of testimonies gathered just after the war's end. The closer to the events the testimony was written, the more we may feel the child's voice is likely to be fully present. However, once more the very process of presenting such material in published form inevitably interferes with such immediacy. My example here is Henryk Grynberg's edited collection, *Children of Zion*. In *Children of Zion*, Grynberg has assembled material from interviews gathered in Palestine in 1943; he describes his role as one of 'selecting and arranging'.[16] The interviewees were the 'Tehran Children': these were young, often orphaned Polish Jews who had been deported to Siberia in 1940 and were allowed to leave for Palestine through Iran a year later. Grynberg has placed his chosen 'fragments' from these interviews in short, chronologically arranged paragraphs. Each new paragraph represents a new voice, so that the same event is told several times by different children, each of whom is anonymous. For instance, we see below what the children remembered of their deportation to Siberia:

> Even though we were famished, my father would not allow us to eat *treyf* [unkosher] soup.
>
> We received four hundred grams of bread daily, and soup – which we did not eat because it was *treyf*.
>
> My father would not eat the soup because it was *treyf*.[17]

As we can see, although each voice is that of a child remembering recent events in their own words, the effect of placing the anonymous voices side by side in this way is literary and not documentary. The children are individuals but repeat the same information and phrases; we get a sense of a collective tragedy but not of unmediated voices.

The effect of multi-voiced interference of this kind is even clearer in the category of the memoir. As memoirs are written retrospectively, we might expect the adult narrator to try to recreate the voice of the child in the past. The first example is from *Hidden*, a testimony by an American brother and sister who were once Polish teenagers Faiga and Luzer Rosenbluth. In this text the children's voices do at first appear to be present. Although the text is a reconstruction, written by a ghost-writer from the life histories of adults Fay and Leo, it uses a stylised, present tense 'image'[18] of teenage idiom. This impression of orality conforms both to the genre of oral Holocaust testimony, and, in literary terms, to Mikhail Bakhtin's notion of 'skaz'. Bakhtin defines this as a mode of narration 'that imitates the oral speech of an individualized narrator'.[19] For instance, Luzer's inner monologue in the barn where he hid during the war consists of a clash of discourses arising from the Polish story and its telling by an American ghost-writer:

> Yeah, yeah, Mamche ordered me to stay alive, to carry on the family name. (Which is pretty funny, since I've changed my first name to Lonek, to seem more Polish.) But, at this minute, I'm like Esau, so hungry … that he'd sell his birthright to Jacob.[20]

Here, skaz consists both of an image of pre-war Jewish idiom (the word 'Mamche', Biblical references), and contemporary American discourse ('Yeah, yeah', 'pretty funny'). Together, they produce not a sample of the child's language itself, but a literary image of one that never existed.

By contrast, in her testimony of hiding in a French convent, Leah Iglinsky-Goodman does at times attempt to reproduce authentically both the perspective and the language of the three-year-old child in a convent cellar:

> I was all alone in this dungeon place. The giant stone walls concealed frightening monsters, and the ceiling, the floor and the huge wooden door …[21]

However, this effort at reproduction is just as stylised as that in *Hidden*, showing the adult narrator's efforts to convey the child's viewpoint (the walls' concealment of 'monsters' is presented as fact) rather than her *voice*. The closer the text tries to approach this voice, the further away it gets, as shown by the use of the unchildlike word 'concealed'. An adult narrator is apparent here, not a child protagonist. The reader knows that the impression of a child's voice in these cases is an adult reconstruction. But, as I have argued, this layering of voices is a positive effect and allows us to read the texts for narrative effect as much as for factual evidence.

My next examples are two memoirs which, in contrast to *Hidden* and *For Love of Life*, suppress any trace of the child's original voice. These are Cordelia Edvardson's *The Burned Child Seeks the Fire*, and Karen Gershon's *A Lesser Child*. Both eschew the first person and instead use third-person narration to convey an abrupt severing of ties between past and present. Gershon's memoir was written in German and translated into English – despite the fact that this was the language she had spoken since she was 15. Rather than acting as the child's language, however, the use of German shows the great gap between the pre-war life of the child Kate Löwenthal and the adult Karen Gershon.

Gershon left Germany for Britain in 1938 on a *Kindertransport* train; although she and her two sisters survived the war, her parents

Paul and Selma Löwenthal were killed. In *A Lesser Child* the limited developmental view of a child is matched by the restricted historical view of someone living in Germany in the 1930s. For instance, the child interpreted her parents' behaviour according only to the familial scenarios of paternal philandering and maternal hysteria, but the adult sees the historical dimension, which the child could not. As we can see in the extract below, Kate's father often stayed out late:

> The cause of Selma's anxiety at such times *may not have been*, as Kate believed, his philandering, but his reckless tongue: he would tell political jokes without caring who might overhear him. When she observed her mother weeping in his arms, this *may not have been*, as she believed, evidence of a reconciliation after a quarrel. Paul may have been trying to comfort her when she was in despair over their worsening circumstances.[22] (emphasis added)

This extract consists of an adult perspective and not the child's voice, shown by the third-person narration. As the phrase of reconstruction shows ('may not have been'), there is an overlap in Holocaust narratives between what Dominick LaCapra calls 'structural or existential trauma'[23] – which is, here, the child's Oedipal view of her parents – and the 'historical trauma' of specific events. Such a historical perspective can only be supplied with hindsight. A similar awareness of historical trauma appears in Edvardson's memoir *The Burned Child Seeks the Fire*. Like the unnamed child in this memoir, Edvardson was born in 1929, the illegitimate daughter of the 'half-Jewish' German writer Elisabeth Langgässer and a Jewish father whom she never met. Although she was brought up as a Catholic, the child was deported to Auschwitz in 1943, partly as the result of her efforts to protect her mother. The 'existential' trauma of the child's familial relationships is inseparable throughout *The Burned Child* from its historical dimension. The child remembers that a family friend called her a '"filthy Jewish brat"' when she was about nine. Only with some effort does the adult narrator recall the incident fully, apparently during the very act of writing:

> What was he so mad about? She no longer knows. But she does! It occurs to her – wasn't that how it was? – that the girl and the blue-eyed son had played forbidden games and been caught. Yes, that's how it was. Yes, she was a filthy Jewish brat.[24]

This extract, like that from *A Lesser Child*, uses third-person narration to convey adult perspective at the expense of the child's view, let alone her voice. Beneath the historicised, racial slur, which Edvardson describes, lies a sexual transgression. However, as in Gershon's memoir, the two are not separable, as the word 'forbidden' suggests: these 'games' represent both an existential and a historically specific affront. Although we seem to read the voice of a child speaking about herself – 'Yes, she was a filthy Jewish brat' – 'she' here is the third-person pronoun chosen by the adult narrator, rather than the child, writing about her younger self. Once more, there is no real trace of the child's voice. The child's *perspective*, however, does remain, in her view of pure Catholicism versus filthy, sexualised Judaism, as she thinks about herself in the third person: 'A filthy Jewish brat: what is that, anyway? Does it mean ... playing forbidden games? But she's really a pious little Catholic girl who took her first communion several years ago'.[25] In both Gershon's and Edvardson's memoirs, the use of third-person narration, rather than the more usual first-person, simply emphasises the formal absence of the child's voice and its replacement by an adult's viewpoint.

Fiction

A fourth category is that of novels by former child survivors. Here the representation of a child's voice is at its least unified, and most literary. I will discuss three examples from this genre. The first is Jona Oberski's novel *A Childhood*, which follows the author's experiences – at the age of five he was deported from the Netherlands to Bergen-Belsen; both his parents died during the war. Most of Oberski's novel concerns an unnamed child who cannot fully understand what is happening around him, but in one chapter it is the *reader* who cannot understand, due to the use of a child's viewpoint. In Belsen, the boy's mother insists that he help carry the empty cooking pots back to the kitchen and clean them out, even though he is too small to reach the pot's handle. In the kitchen,

> All the children bent over the edges of the pots. Some couldn't keep their feet on the ground. All I could see were their backs and legs. Their heads and arms were gone. I would have liked to help with the cleaning, but I didn't know how.[26]

When the children are asked if they enjoyed the food, the boy says, 'I'd had my head in the pot so long that I hadn't noticed anything good being handed out'.[27] It is only at this point that it becomes clear to the adult reader that the boy was sent to 'help' in the kitchen in order to lick out the cooking pots, and, predictably, the boy's mother is angry with him for not eating the extra food. The act of misunderstanding is extended through the use of a child's viewpoint, as we can see in the extract describing – but not labelling – the children licking out the cooking pots. However, even here it is not the child's voice that we hear directly, but its mediation, through that of a scarcely perceptible adult narrator who relates this episode in the present. The adult narrator uses deliberately simple language and short sentences in a *stylisation*,[28] rather than a reproduction, of the child's voice. This is not realism so much as adherence to the literary convention I mentioned above, common in novels about children, which invariably separates character and focaliser even as they appear to be united in first-person utterance.[29]

The second example is from Henryk Grynberg's autobiographical novel *Child of the Shadows*. Like Grynberg himself, the boy Henryk in the novel lived on false Aryan papers in Warsaw with his mother from the age of six. Once more, an apparent reproduction of a child's voice also includes the adult narrator's, as we see in an episode where Henryk and his mother walk down the street pretending to be Aryan. The adult narrator describes the boy's perception: 'Mama was walking next to me and even smiling. But her smile was of the kind I could still remember from the days when we went visiting. Therefore, we must be visiting, I thought'.[30] Unlike the episode about the cooking pots from Oberski's *A Childhood*, here the adult reader knows perfectly well what the truth of the matter is. Henryk's mother has an artificial smile on her face, which the boy can only comprehend in terms of a vanished social world; he is too young to understand, and can only adapt to, the demands of passing for gentile. Yet in both cases it is the child's perspective and not his voice that we read. This is despite the fact that, within the adult narration, Grynberg preserves childlike diction ('Mama', 'went visiting'). In the pattern with which we are now familiar, however, it is the adult's voice that is uppermost, relating the experiences of his childhood self.

Finally, a particularly unusual fictional example of a child's-eye view of the Holocaust years is Raymond Federman's experimental novella *The Voice in the Closet*. This autobiographical novel is about the day of the great round up in Paris on 14 July 1942, when his mother pushed the 13-year-old boy into a wardrobe. He thus avoided the fate of his family, which was deportation to death in Auschwitz, and instead emigrated to the US. Throughout, the narration in *The Voice* shifts pronoun, so that it is often hard to tell whether boy or adult is speaking, as the opening lines show:

> here now again selectricstud makes me speak with its balls all balls foutaise sam says in his closet upstairs but this time it's going to be serious ... yesterday a rock flew through the windowpane ... scared the hell out of him as he waits for me to unfold upstairs.[31]

Unlike all the other examples I have mentioned, here it is the child in the past who talks about the adult in the present – '*he* waits for *me* to unfold'. Yet the child in *The Voice* always emphasises the impossibility of retrieving the voice or experience of the adult writer's younger self. The child mockingly calls the adult 'selectricstud': he is a writer using a Selectric golfball typewriter with fonts for different languages on changeable balls, which produces only rubbish ('all balls'). The adult writer is a fan of 'Sam' – Samuel Beckett – and the child ironically quotes the French word for 'rubbish', '*foutaise*', which is what he predicts the outcome of the adult's 'serious' autobiographical impulse will be. But of course once more this is a literary conceit, because the experience and the voice of the child who Federman once was are indeed lost forever. The two voices represent an internal, spatial debate, which takes place within the adult writer's consciousness, rather than a temporal link to a past self. Throughout, the novel is about the adult writer's failure to recapture the traumatic childhood moment. Child and adult act alternately as narrator and focaliser, something possible only in a fictional narrative from which any 'authentic' child's voice is absent.

Conclusion

In conclusion, we can see that Holocaust literature from a child's viewpoint cannot make use of an unmediated child's voice. But the interference of other voices, particularly those of an adult narrator, editor, or even reader, actually adds to the child's text. Many voices multiply the text's temporal and spatial elements, as well as conveying – through the absence of a unitary child's voice – the reality of that absence and loss in children's Holocaust texts.

NOTES

1. Binjamin Wilkomirski, *Fragments: Memories of a Childhood, 1939–1948*, trans. Carol Brown Janeway (London: Picador, 1996 [1995]). See Stefan Maechler's full account of the controversy, *The Wilkomirski Affair: A Study in Biographical Truth*, trans. John E. Woods (New York: Schocken, 2001).
2. See also Sue Vice, *Children Writing the Holocaust* (Basingstoke: Palgrave, 2004).
3. Norman Geras, *The Contract of Mutual Indifference: Political Philosophy after the Holocaust* (London: Verso, 1998), p.81.
4. Shlomith Rimmon-Kenan, *Narrative Fiction: Contemporary Poetics* (London: Methuen, 1983), p.72.
5. Shlomo Breznitz, *Memory Fields: The Legacy of a Wartime Childhood in Czechoslovakia* (New York: Alfred A. Knopf, 1993), p.80.
6. Louis Begley, *Wartime Lies* (London: Picador, 1991), pp.115–16.
7. Mary Berg, *Warsaw Ghetto: A Diary*, trans. Norbert Guterman, ed. S.L. Shneiderman (New York: L.B. Fisher, 1945), pp.75–7.
8. Ibid., p.216.
9. See Alexandra Zapruder, *Salvaged Pages: Young Writers' Diaries of the Holocaust* (New Haven and London: Yale University Press, 2002), pp.445–6.
10. Éva Heyman, *The Diary of Éva Heyman*, trans. Moshe M. Kohn (New York: Shapolsky, 1973).
11. Hanno Loewy and Andrjez Bodek (eds.), *'Les Vrais Riches' – Notizen am Rand: Ein Tagebuch aus dem Ghetto Lódz (Mai bis August 1944)*, trans. Esther Alexander-Ihme *et al.* (Leipzig: Reclam, 1997), entry for 15 July 1944, p.74. The boy wrote this entry in English.
12. Ibid., p.51, entry for 26 June 1944, originally written in Polish.
13. Yitskhok Rudashevski, *The Diary of the Vilna Ghetto*, trans. Percy Matenko (Israel: Ghetto Fighters' House, 1973), p.28.
14. Ibid., p.120.
15. Anne Frank, *The Diary of a Young Girl: The Definitive Edition*, trans. and ed. Susan Massotty, Otto H. Frank and Mirjam Pressler (New York: Bantam Books, 1995 [1947]), pp.73, 138, 182.
16. Henryk Grynberg (ed.), *Children of Zion*, trans. Jacqueline Mitchell (Evanston, IL: Northwestern University Press, 1997), p.xi.
17. Ibid., p.79.
18. This is Mikhail Bakhtin's term, from his essay 'Discourse in the Novel', *The Dialogic Imagination: Four Essays*, trans. Caryl Emerson and Michael Holquist (Austin, TX: University of Texas Press, 1981), p.336.
19. Mikhail Bakhtin, *Problems of Dostoevsky's Poetics*, trans. Caryl Emerson (Minneapolis, MN: University of Minnesota Press, 1984), p.8.
20. Fay Walker and Leo Rosen, with Caren S. Neile, *Hidden: A Sister and Brother in Nazi Poland* (Madison, WI: University of Wisconsin Press, 2002), pp.9–10.
21. Leah Iglinski-Goodman, *For Love of Life* (London: Vallentine Mitchell, 2002), p.1.
22. Karen Gershon, *A Lesser Child: An Autobiography*, trans. unnamed (London: Peter Owen, 1992), p.102.
23. Dominick LaCapra, *History and Memory after Auschwitz* (Ithaca, NY: Cornell University Press, 1998), p.47.

24. Cordelia Edvardson, *The Burned Child Seeks the Fire: A Memoir*, trans. Joel Agee (Boston: Beacon Press, 1997 [1984]), p.18.
25. Ibid., p.19.
26. Jona Oberski, *A Childhood: A Novella*, trans. Ralph Manheim (London: Hodder and Stoughton, 1983 [1978]), p.46.
27. Ibid., p.47.
28. This is also Bakhtin's term, meaning a formal, literary imitation of extra-literary 'everyday narration', Bakhtin, 'Discourse in the Novel', p.262.
29. See Rimmon-Kenan's discussion of this technique in relation to the opening of James Joyce's *A Portrait of the Artist as a Young Man*, in *Narrative Fiction*, pp.72–3.
30. Henryk Grynberg, *Child of the Shadows*, trans. Celina Wieniewska (London: Vallentine Mitchell, 1969), p.70.
31. Raymond Federman, *The Voice in the Closet/La Voix dans le Cabinet de Débarras* (Madison, WI: Coda Press 1979), unnumbered pages.

Drawing the Holocaust in 1945

NICHOLAS STARGARDT

In the early summer of 1945, the Swiss Red Cross invited 300 child survivors of the camps to recuperate in Switzerland for a few months.[1] Many of the children came from Buchenwald. Among them were two Jewish boys of 16: Kalman Landau was Polish, Thomas Geve, German. Both had survived Auschwitz, Buchenwald and the evacuation marches to Gross Rosen in the snows of January 1945, and during that year both drew pictures to illustrate their experiences. A cycle of Landau's 12 pictures would be published in the Swiss magazine *Du* in March 1946; Geve's had to wait another 50 years, mainly for family reasons, before Yad Vashem and the Gedenkstätte Buchenwald brought them into public view. About Thomas Geve we know a good deal; about Kalman Landau very little. But in their different ways, each also left clues about themselves in the art works they produced.[2]

In his cycle of 12 pictures Kalman Landau chronicled his passage from being driven into the *Lager* from a passenger train, through roll call in the camp, forced labour, 'organising' food (that is, stealing provisions to supplement the starvation rations), the execution of prisoners who had attempted to escape, the gas chamber, the shooting and clubbing of prisoners in the snow during the forced marches to Groß-Rosen, the further transports through the wind and snow in open goods wagons, and then the cramming of thousands of prisoners together in the quarantine barracks on arrival. Finally, the last two pictures tell of the disarming and arrest of the Buchenwald SS guards by the prisoners and Kalman's arrival at the Swiss border in a railway train very similar to the one which had originally brought him to the camps. And even here there is barbed wire at the border post – as there probably was in reality.

Landau was a Polish Jew and, although he chose German for the captions, it was probably his third language, replicating the slang and commands of the concentration camp, as well as the language of his carers and teachers in Switzerland in 1945. Everywhere his effort to

1a. Kalman Landau, 'Wir organisier[e]n'; and 1b. '3 Heftlinge ferurteilt zum Galgen' (reproduced courtesy of *Du* magazine, Zurich) [NB the German in the captions throughout is Landau's].

2a. Kalman Landau, 'Apel!!!'; and 2b. 'So gehen wir kaputt' (reproduced courtesy of *Du* magazine, Zurich).

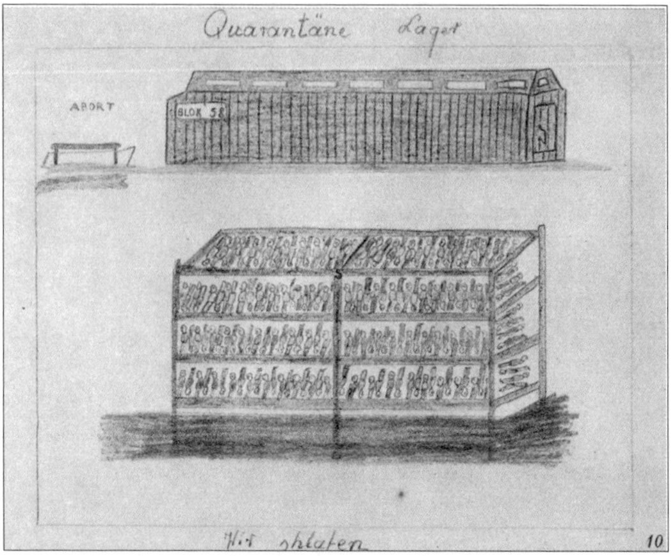

3. Kalman Landau, 'Quarantäne Lager' (reproduced courtesy of *Du* magazine, Zurich).

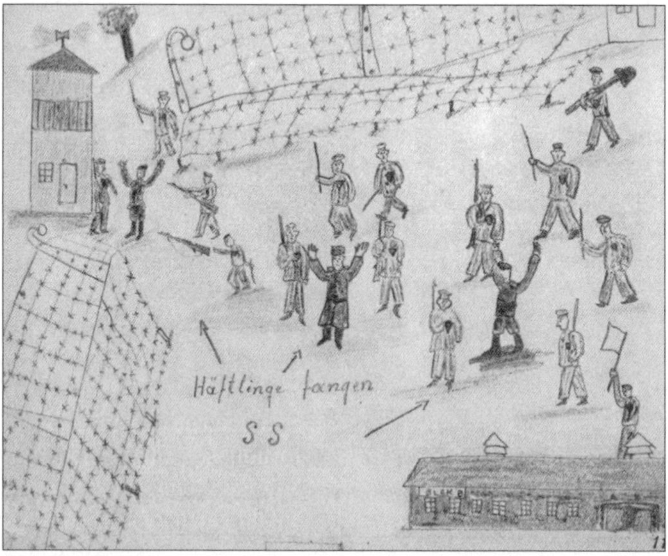

4. Kalman Landau, 'Häftlinge fangen SS' (reproduced courtesy of *Du* magazine, Zurich).

control the line and capture the detail is evident, whether the prisoners are searching for supplies before the evacuation marches set out, or he is showing how two stools were piled on top of each other under the feet of prisoners about to be hanged on the gallows (see 1a. 'Wir organisier[e]n', and 1b. '3 Heftlinge ferurteilt zum Galgen).

There are some elements to the story telling which are universal amongst children and acquire their particular significance in the context of ghetto or camp. Having started work on children's pictures from the Holocaust by looking at some of the 4,000 drawings and paintings which survive from the Jewish ghetto in Theresienstadt, I found myself looking back at them for clues as to how children's artistic imaginations were formed. In Theresienstadt, the food queue became a form of primary socialisation for new arrivals, as well as a source of endless complaints, charges and counter-charges of corrupt practice among adults. Children routinely followed the bread cart through the ghetto streets and witnessed the struggle for existence into which the food queue drove most adults. Whereas in Theresienstadt, it is the ghetto police and the cooks ladling out the rations at the soup kitchens who tower over the hapless adults and children queuing up to receive them, in Landau's drawings of the concentration camps it is the SS guards, the *kapos* (prisoner functionaries) and the doctors who have recognisable features. And the rifle butt used to club the stragglers on the march through the snow is enormous (see 2a. 'Apel!!!', and 2b. 'So gehen wir kaputt').[3]

The prisoners – presumably including Landau himself – are indistinguishable from one another, so many powerless, interchangeable '*Stücke*' to be marched, stored and killed. Crammed into the quadruple bunks of the 'Quarantine barracks' they have no identity at all (see 3. 'Quarantäne Lager'). Only when the prisoners regain some autonomy and 'organise' things in the camp or on the march westwards do they become individual and distinct. But even at the end when armed Buchenwald prisoners arrest the SS, the guards are still bigger and more detailed than the camp prisoners. It would take more than liberation to overcome their power (see 4. 'Häftlinge fangen SS').

Landau's artistic technique oscillates between that of a younger child and that of an adult, testifying to the tension between recovering the techniques learned in a pre-war childhood to depict the events which had put paid to practising the skill any further. In

5a. Kalman Landau, 'Von Heimat ins Lager'; and 5b. 'Wir gehn zu Arbeit' (reproduced courtesy of *Du* magazine, Zurich).

the enclosed spaces, this panoptic vision is disclosed by the use of cut away techniques. Both the quarantine barracks and the gas chamber are shown from the outside, in order to locate what is happening within them. At the same time, the prisoners marching to work in the iron foundry might, in different circumstances, have been a child's depiction of children on a hike with their teacher. The trees here, like those in all the other camp pictures by Landau, are identical (see 5a. 'Von Heimat ins Lager', and 5b. 'Wir gehn zu Arbeit').

Over the deadly roll call, continued into the freezing darkness, ride the crescent moon and stars of any young child's picture. Yet, Landau feels no need to draw the engine for any of his three trains, and confidently cuts away the crematorium building, with all the mastery of a much older boy.

Another element, which I think is more typical of boys' than girls' drawings, is to be found in Landau's spatial mapping. He strives not for due proportions, but for an overview of the entire scene and the logical relationship of its parts. Landau added signs or captions to make the logic of his scenes unmistakeable: 'Morgen Tempo' (Morning march), 'Zum Krematorium' (To the crematorium), 'Block Äl[te]ster' (Block elder), 'Es stimmt' (It tallies) and – more ominously in the late night roll call – 'Es stimmt nicht' (The numbers don't tally). In the Theresienstadt ghetto, boys like Josef Kraus drew the newly constructed railway sidings, focusing upon mechanical contraptions in works devoid of people.[4] Thomas Geve's work is also striking in this regard. He set out to explain how the camps functioned, by delineating how the barrack blocks were constructed and how the building *Kommando* on which he had worked in Auschwitz sub-divided its tasks (see 6. 'So arbeiten wir').

He drew the armbands of all the different ranks of prisoner functionaries and the process by which new arrivals progressed through the different sections of the camp. As a boy in Berlin, he had admired the junctions of the Berlin *S-Bahn* and Nazi exhibitions of French war booty for their application of engineering and technology. As a future building engineer himself, his art dwelt upon the technical aspects of installations and the technical division of labour within the camps, often to the exclusion of the people.[5]

In their different ways, each of these boys was concerned with representing experience in terms of a kind of spatial mapping, in which they dwelt on how things worked rather than on the individual

6. Thomas Geve, 'So arbeiten wir' (No.32, Collection of the Yad Vashem Art Museum).

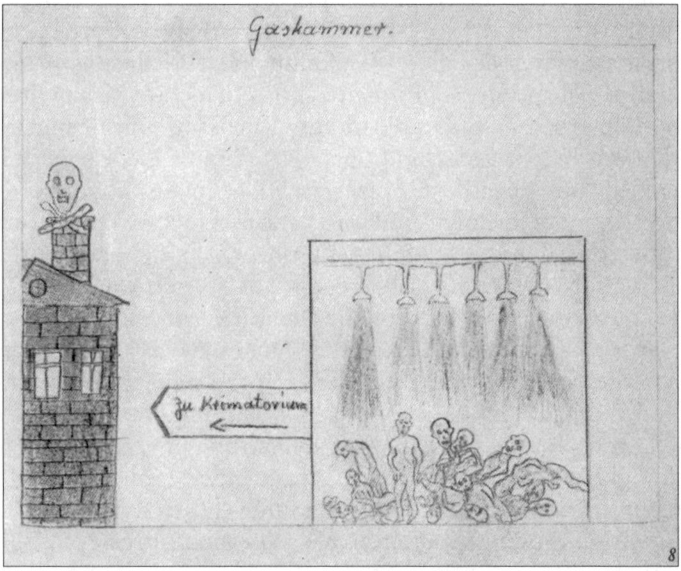

7. Kalman Landau, 'Gaskammer' (reproduced courtesy of *Du* magazine, Zurich).

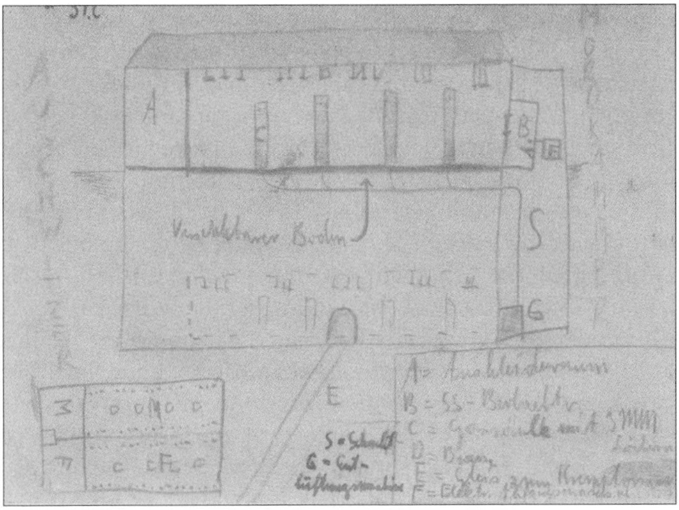

8. Thomas Geve, 'Auschwitzer Mordkammer' (No.35, Collection of the Yad Vashem Art Museum).

9. Thomas Geve, 'Es mahnen uns die Toten der Konzentrationslager' (No.1, Collection of the Yad Vashem Art Museum).

or the psychological dimensions of experience. A small group of Czech boys who produced a weekly journal, *Vedem*, in the Theresienstadt ghetto, recorded their 'Rambles through Terezin'. The goals of their first visits included the morgue and the newly built crematorium.[6] There may have been nothing more in their account of the workings and capacity of the crematorium than a boyish enthusiasm for technological mastery as well as an adolescent fascination with the fate of the dead. We have to remember that they knew nothing of the gas chambers and incinerators of Auschwitz-Birkenau in which most of them would eventually perish.

Both Landau and Geve also felt that they should try to illustrate the gas chambers of Auschwitz-Birkenau, even though neither had seen them, as if neither of their accounts of survival could be complete without this central element of the death camps (see 7. 'Gaskammer', and 8. 'Auschwitzer Mordkammer'). Looking at these pictures in 2004, Geve was still struck by the technical inaccuracy of placing the lift to the crematorium inside the gas chamber itself: such a mistake, stemming from trying to visualise what he had not witnessed, went against his dedication to exact detail. He also explained that he did not trust himself to draw the prisoners inside. In any case, depicting the mechanics of control may have provided the vehicle Geve needed for channelling his emotions: it was as if he already knew that he would become an engineer.

The drawings of the two teenagers have parallels. Landau's depiction of the liberation of Buchenwald rotates a similar drawing in which Geve carefully tried to locate the position of the American tanks outside the perimeter and main gate as accurately as he could. The skull Landau placed atop of the crematorium chimney is reminiscent of the skull Geve had placed at the centre of his depiction of the entire camp system. But whereas Geve's pictures worked through strong geometric arrangements, Landau's revolved around the events. Geve's skull represented an enclosed system of mass killing; in Landau's drawing, it chronicled an unfolding tale (see 9. 'Es mahnen uns die Toten der Konzentrationslager').

These parallels were not entirely accidental. In the Swiss children's home on the mountain above Zug where Landau drew his pictures in the summer of 1945, Geve's work served as a model. By this point, Thomas Geve had already drawn well over a hundred pictures of the camps, and they were passed from hand to hand and used to encourage the other children to express themselves through pictures, as the care workers saw that art could serve as therapy.[7]

Geve had begun drawing in Buchenwald during the weeks immediately following his liberation, while he was regaining weight and too weak to go out of his barracks. One of the German communist prisoners whom he had befriended brought him a pad of blue Nazi forms. As his mania for drawing scenes from camp life became known, many inmates crowded to see his work and bring him the stubs of coloured pencils. Thomas Geve wanted to create a visual encyclopaedia of the camps for his father. As he started to draw on the block of blue forms in Buchenwald, they reminded him of the cigarette cards he used to collect in pre-war Berlin.[8]

Thomas's father had gone to Britain in 1939, expecting his family to join him once he had made arrangements. During those last months before the war broke out, he had maintained contact with his ten-year-old son in Berlin by pandering to his craze about cigarette cards and sending him English ones he had not seen. Assembling collections of cigarette cards amounted to gathering the minute pieces of an encyclopaedia devoted to a particular theme: often the series might run to 200 cards. The idea that the world could be divided into such capsules of information would profoundly influence Thomas. At the end of the war, when he started to pick up the threads of his life again in Buchenwald, he would turn to this idea as he looked for a way to share his knowledge with his father once more. But there were no cigarette cards to describe the world from which he was emerging: he would have to make his own. This was a world of which his father had no idea, and in which his mother had perished. And true to the model of the cigarette-card encyclopaedia, his cycle of drawings followed the logic of the world of the camps, rather than tracing his own personal history and emotional experience. It was also a project Geve was able to bring to fruition: when he reached England, he gave the pictures to his father.[9]

* * *

Kalman Landau and Thomas Geve were each attempting to depict camp life and the death marches in their matter-of-fact horror. Both were emotionally restrained and both show a clear separation between that world and this. In Geve's drawings, the world of the camps is a separate system, a world enclosed and sufficient to itself. In Landau's, the very clarity of his chronological sequence, from his arrival at the camp at the beginning, testified to his clear recognition of its eventual end. It was a classic social narrative, whose closeness to events made it easy to chart and grasp, though it is harder to know what it meant to the artist himself. This sense of separation sets the immediate post-war drawings of Geve and Landau apart from works like the Theresienstadt drawings, which were produced in the midst of the Holocaust. Sometimes it is as if we were intruding in the midst of a disturbance, a working out of a rupture between the pre-ghetto time and the ghetto present, as the different elements of each crowd into the same picture. They did not know where they were bound next, and when they did learn that they were going to Auschwitz-Birkenau they had no idea what awaited them there. Often they looked back on the homes they had lost as a golden age, rather than imagining the future utopias their teachers tried to encourage. Few of the Theresienstadt child artists lived to see liberation. In Kalman Landau's and Thomas Geve's cycles we see a first – and an emotionally restrained – attempt by survivors to tell their tales. Instinctively, each reached back to ways of telling he already knew, be it the episodic journey or the encyclopaedia. But both knew too that they were telling them to audiences who had not been there.

NOTES

1. See, for instance, Charlotte Weber, *Gegen den Strom der Finsternis: Als Betreuerin in Schweizer Flüchtlingsheimen 1942–1945* (Zürich: Chronos, 1997).
2. Kalman Landau, reproduced in *Du* magazine, March 1946. I am grateful to the editors of *Du* magazine for permission to reproduce these drawings here. Thomas Geve, *Es gibt hier keine Kinder: Auschwitz, Gross-Rosen, Buchenwald: Zeichnungen eines kindlichen Historikers*, ed. Volkhard Knigge (Göttingen: Wallstein, 1997). On children who survived the concentration camps, see Dorothy Macardle, *Children of Europe: A Study of the Children of Liberated Countries: Their War-time Experiences, their Reactions, and their Needs, with a Note on Germany* (London: Gollancz, 1949); Kyrił Sosnowski, *The Tragedy of Children under Nazi Rule* (Poznań: Zachodnia Agencja Prasowa, 1962); Sarah Moskovitz, *Love despite Hate: Child Survivors of the Holocaust and their Adult Lives* (New York: Schocken Books, 1983); Martin Gilbert, *The Boys: Triumph over Adversity* (London: Phoenix, 1996); and Nicholas Stargardt, *Witnesses of War: Children's Lives under the Nazis* (London: Jonathan Cape, 2005), esp. ch.12.
3. See Nicholas Stargardt, 'Children's Art of the Holocaust', *Past and Present*, No.161 (1998), pp.192–235.
4. In Theresienstadt, boys drew the factories and a whole railway system in pictures

where the relationship of space, buildings and mechanical objects was paramount: see Archive of the Jewish Museum in Prague, cat. no.121.521 (Josef Kraus), and cat. no.129.005 (anon).

5. Thomas Geve, interview with author and public lecture, Southampton, January 2004. See also his 1958 memoir, *Youth in Chains* (Jerusalem: R. Mass, 1981), pp.15–21; and Geve, *Es gibt hier keine Kinder*, pp.10–11.
6. Petr Ginz, 'Rambles through Terezín' (1943), in Marie Rút Křížková, Kurt Jiří Kotouč and Zdeněk Ornest (eds.), *We Are Children Just the Same: Vedem, the Secret Magazine of the Boys of Terezín* (Philadelphia: Jewish Publication Society, 1995), pp.85–7.
7. Geve, interview with author, Southampton, January 2004.
8. Ibid. See also Stargardt, *Witnesses of War*, p.30.
9. Geve, interview with author, Southampton, January 2004.

Stolen Childhood: Austrian Romany Ceija Stojka and her Past

SUSAN TEBBUTT

This transition time, when we were in the concentration camp, this time has gone. It was stolen from us ... For the finest part of childhood, when others were playing with dolls, I – and my little brother – were having to break and carry the heavy stones. For our little Ossi it was too much. He perished in Auschwitz.[1]

Ceija Stojka

Austrian Lovara Romany Ceija Stojka does not want to forget what she and her family suffered during the National Socialist period, and through her memoirs and art has created a testimony which has resonance not only for Romanies, but for all Austrians, and all those who are concerned that never again should innocent children be robbed of their entitlement to a tranquil childhood.

At the age of 11 Ceija was one of those internees at Bergen-Belsen concentration camp fortunate enough to be liberated by British troops on 15 April 1945. Although as a Romany she had been banned by the National Socialists from attending school, after the end of the war she went back to learn the basic skills of reading and writing. It was, however, not until over 40 years later that she was encouraged by the journalist Karin Berger to publish her memoirs. In *Wir leben im Verborgenen* (We Live Hidden Lives),[2] Ceija Stojka writes of her concentration camp experiences, setting these memories in the context of her life prior to the persecution of the Romanies, life in a close-knit family which formed part of a much larger extended group of families travelling around in Austria with horse and wagon until 1939. She writes without bitterness, recalling the mood of the times, and placing great emphasis on the importance of her family and religion. Today the Madonna plays an important role in her daily life.

1. Ceija Stojka in front of the Madonna in her Vienna home, 2004.[3]

Wir leben im Verborgenen was followed in 1992 by *Reisende auf dieser Welt* (Traveller in This World).[4] Both include interviews with Ceija Stojka conducted by journalist Karin Berger.[5] Whereas her first volume focused primarily on experiences of the Third Reich, the second is concerned more with the post-war years, her coming to terms with the past, and promoting the Romany culture. She is frequently invited as a Holocaust survivor to speak at memorial sites, schools and cultural centres.

Since she is one of the very few Romany women survivors who have written their memoirs, it is fitting that in the US Holocaust Memorial Museum in Washington, DC her story is one of those used for the 'identity cards' which visitors receive when they enter the museum. Visitors learn at various stages of the exhibition what 'their' person was experiencing, and discover at the end whether he or she has survived. This means that rather than merely absorb empty statistics, visitors are given an opportunity to identify with a real person.

Ceija Stojka has also expressed her feelings in poetry and art, and in 2003 a volume was published entitled *Meine Wahl zu schreiben – Ich kann es nicht* (My Choice to Write – I Have None).[6] It contains poems in German (including Austrian dialect), some of which are translated into Romani (the language of the Romanies), and reproductions of her paintings. Since a visit to Hiroshima in the late 1980s Ceija Stojka has been extremely busy painting. Exhibitions of her work have been held in Germany, England, Japan and Austria, with a major show from December 2004 to March 2005 in the Simon Wiesenthal rooms at the Jewish Museum in Vienna. The creator of powerful images of both rural life and the horrors of the Nazi regime is gradually gaining the recognition she deserves,[7] not least thanks to Karin Berger, who in 1999 devoted an 85-minute documentary film to Ceija Stojka's life and work.[8]

Before looking at the written and graphic depictions of her childhood, and the shadow that her internment and experiences under the Nazis cast over the rest of her life, it is important to locate her experiences in their historical context.

Marginalisation of the Romanies in Holocaust Studies

Between half a million and a million European Romanies perished during the Third Reich, yet the history of the Romanies, or 'Gypsies', is generally relegated to footnote status within Holocaust Studies.

The few existing studies, notably those by Kenrick and Puxon (1981), Crowe and Kolsti (1991), Zimmermann (1996), Wippermann (1997) and Lewy (2000),[9] focus primarily on the historical perspective of the genocide of the Romanies.

There are many accounts of children of the Holocaust, but very few of Romany children. *Die Kinder von Auschwitz* (The Children of Auschwitz), Alwin Meyer's moving collection of 13 personal stories, does include a few paragraphs on the Gypsy camp in the introduction, but has no personal account of a Romany child.[10] The Documentation Centre for German Sinti and Roma in Heidelberg published a volume devoted entirely to the fate of children under the Nazis, including analyses of aspects of the National Socialist policy on the annihilation of Sinti and Roma children. It includes two short testimonies by Herbert Adler and Else Baker about their experiences as Romany children.[11] One of the few substantial records of Romany childhood, which has been translated into English, is Otto Rosenberg's *A Gypsy in Auschwitz*.[12] There are few written records of Romanies' experiences, partly because Romani is primarily a spoken language and has no standard written form, and also because until recently the majority of Romanies did not complete their secondary education. Of the existing records, the majority are by men.[13] The Stojka family therefore stands out because three members, Karl, Mongo and Ceija, have recorded their childhood experiences in writing and art.

In 1994 Ceija's brother Karl (1931–2003), survivor of Auschwitz, Buchenwald and Flossenbürg, published his memories of the Nazi years and his later travels.[14] The three main exhibition catalogues of his paintings of his camp experiences are *Ein Kind in Birkenau*, *Gas* and *Mein Name im Dritten Reich: Z 5742*.[15] Exhibitions of his work have been held in many countries, including Austria, England, France, Germany, Hungary, the Netherlands, Poland and the US.[16] In 1999 he was given the honorary title of professor for his services to art and the Romany world.

In 2000 Ceija's brother Mongo (1929–) published a volume of his memories, *Papierene Kinder* (Paper Children), which in turn includes quite a number of references to Karl's earlier account.[17]

It is Ceija, however, who communicates her recollections, responses and exhortations to her audience through the widest range of different media (prose, poetry, oral interviews and art), and who adds a new dimension to the cultural history of children and the Holocaust. Her autobiographical testimony may be seen in the context of Austrian women's writing, and is a good example of what Homi Bhabha describes as the hybridity of cultures,[18] since Ceija clearly has a tripartite identity as an Austrian, a woman and a Romany.[19] A further dimension is added by the fact that during the Nazi period Ceija was but a child, a child whose childhood was effectively stolen from her.

Drawing on the two written autobiographical accounts and the accompanying published interviews relating to them,[20] the 2003 collection of poetry, and the interviews I myself conducted with Ceija in 1998 and 2004, I would like to analyse the key role which her stolen, traumatic childhood played in her development, looking first at her prose and poetry, and then at her art.[21]

The Language of Pain

Born on 13 May 1933 in the Steiermark, the fifth of six children, Ceija did not grow up with a culture of books and reading, but as part of a Lovara Romany family where the oral tradition of story telling and singing dominated (see 2. The family wagon in winter).

Her father dealt in horses, her mother made a living reading palms. Because of ever-tightening restrictions on the participation of Romanies in public life, Ceija was not allowed to attend school for long, thus her written accounts could not be recorded on the spot, but are drawn later from her memories of her cataclysmic experiences at the hands of the Nazis in Auschwitz, Ravensbrück and Bergen-Belsen. Similarly, she did not have an idea of the wider picture of the situation of Romanies in Europe at the time, but in later interviews may obviously draw on knowledge acquired later.

> For her the act of writing is painful, because as she writes she relives the trauma 'as if it happened yesterday ... Yet my thoughts run faster than my hands are able to put everything down on paper'.[22]

What is the language she actually puts down on paper? Ceija Stojka is both a Romany and a citizen of a specific European country, Austria, and she grew up bilingual. In *Wir leben im Verborgenen* there are two striking linguistic features. One is that she includes a few Romani words

2. The family wagon in winter.

and expressions, generally when she quotes her mother's reactions in moments of acute danger, often in the form of prayers to God for their survival. The second striking feature of the language, which is difficult to convey in an English translation, is its very 'Austrianness' in terms of morphology and lexis.[23] Ceija Stojka did, after all, grow up in Austria, and the grammatical structures which distinguish Austrian or South German from High German are pervasive, and Austrian diminutive forms and words relating to Austrian specialities to eat or drink are common currency, not to mention the references to specific Austrian towns, villages, suburbs and buildings.

Depicting Family Tragedy

The first tragedy to strike young Ceija came when her father was arrested and taken to Dachau. Her mother then received a letter reporting his death there, upon which she requested that the urn be sent to her. It finally arrived in the post, and the family held a three-day wake, as is the Romany custom. Soon after, the SS arrived at their house with a large lorry and erected a metal fence, which virtually imprisoned the family. New laws prevented them from travelling in Austria, as Gypsies started to be rounded up. Ceija recalls the way her family was treated:

> The first day was extremely sad. We were mourning our father and other mother was crying; she had to keep thinking about the funeral. After all she was now on her own with six children. The next day more and more people came into this room, so there was less and less space. Then the Gestapo came and took away our three brothers, Hansi, Karl and Ossi. They shaved the lads' heads; us sisters sat there and cried.
>
> But it was to get even worse. Nobody could imagine what was going to happen now, what these people planned to do with us. When the room was so full that there was not even room for a mouse, the transport to Auschwitz was organised. We were pressed into a cattle truck, and right at the start I'd lost one of my shoes, which I couldn't find again. It was so full in this truck that I couldn't even bend down. After a very long journey the train finally came to a stop. We begged for water – we were almost dying of thirst and hunger. They calmed us down and said: 'The water is too rusty, maybe you'll get water at the next stop'. And so it went on until we got to Auschwitz.[24]

In her uncompromising style Ceija Stojka gives graphic descriptions of how numbers were tattooed on their arms, hers being Z6399. (When talking in the 1990s and early twenty-first century about her experiences, Ceija comments that when people make ignorant remarks about her still visible tattoo she points out that she does not feel ashamed to display it openly, since it is the Nazi perpetrators who should be ashamed of what they did to a young child.) She describes the exhausting work in the quarry, the inadequate, meagre food rations, the typhoid epidemics, the death of her brother Ossi, and the cruel beating of her brothers Karl and Hansi and her sister Mitzi, when the SS suspected them of stealing a piece of soap. All of this happens against a backdrop of dust, dirt and death:

> We marched to the crematorium. The ground under our feet was very hot, black, human dust. The puddles of dirt on the left-hand side stank more than the dead bodies in our barracks.[25]

After the liquidation of the Gypsy camp in Auschwitz, which Ceija survived by pretending to be 16 and fit for work, she was taken on a transport to Ravensbrück.

Even in the midst of the horrendous experiences there were almost surreal moments, such as the Christmas Eve 1944 celebration at which the children were given cake and hot milk by the guards, sang *Silent Night*, and each received an apple and a few nuts. The description of the arrival in Bergen-Belsen is, however, more typical of the memoir:

> We arrived in Bergen-Belsen camp; it was in the middle of a large forest. We marched through an iron barred gate. The first sight was deeply shocking. A few dead bodies were lying right behind the gate, and their chests were slit open, and their heart and liver were missing. Mama said 'Na da ra murie scheej!' (Don't be afraid, my child.) There were not many barracks in this camp. Just a few paces in front of the barracks the dead bodies were lying, such that you couldn't even count them, one on top of the other, young and old, and some were also still alive. We had to go into a long ugly barracks; there were no box beds in it. The whole barracks was desolate. Windows, well there were none, and on the ground, where there were hardly any planks, lay a few sick people.[26]

The young Ceija not only conveys the pain affecting her own family, but empathises with a woman in Bergen-Belsen whom she recognises as having been a clerical worker in Auschwitz:

> [she] was also there with her son. But her little three-year-old boy was lying on the pile of corpses. He was lying on his back. Beautiful blue eyes he had, and black hair. Over his body was a dark blue angora jersey. He'd been a beautiful child, but now he'd already been dead for eight days. His mother was sitting the whole day in front of this pile of corpses; you could hardly drag her away.[27]

The liberation by the English soldiers is a turning point. Ceija and the other children are given clothes, shoes, coats and hats, and treated in a friendly manner, as befits children not prisoners. But does this mean the end of pain and suffering?

Reflecting on the Consequences of the Genocide of the Romanies

After the end of the war Ceija is all too aware of the decimated ranks of her own and other Romany families, and worried lest the anti-Gypsyism continues.

> I'm often afraid that my children and their children will have to experience as difficult a period of persecution as we did. In any case, they are also still suffering from the former crimes of the Nazis ... But we never want to forget. How could we, anyway? All of us who have survived the horror still lament and cry for our dead. Our children often grew up without a grandmother or grandfather, many without father or mother. And where are their uncles and aunts?[28]

As if the loss of so many family members, and the nightmares about the barbed wire, the screaming and the stink of camp existence had not been bad enough, the persecution did not end with the end of the Nazi regime. Regulations in 1949 in Cologne designed to 'combat the Gypsy nuisance', for example, continued the Nazi restrictions on licences for itinerant Gypsies, and the marginalisation of Romanies in terms of housing and social welfare went side by side with a failure to empathise with Romany survivors.[29] Ceija recalls having the comment hurled at her, 'Well, you've really got a fine telephone number!' when someone noticed the tattooed number on her arm,[30] and recounts how her niece is a good secretary, but keeps her Romany origins quiet for fear of losing her job.[31]

This fear gives an indication of the post-war continuity of anti-Gypsyism, a phenomenon that is not only apparent in psychological terms. Claims made by Sinti and Roma survivors for restitution for incarceration in internment camps were frequently disallowed (the only financial compensation Ceija ever received some ten years after the end of the war was two meagre payments of 15,000 Austrian shillings), and claims for psychological trauma were also usually disregarded. In 2004 Ceija suffered the shock of finding out that the only memory she had of her father's death was in fact a Nazi fabrication:

> Well, as I said, for almost fifty years we thought that he'd in fact died in Dachau. Yes, and then I was here at home and ... got a letter, and that letter was very cautious. Well, at first they didn't want to tell me at all, but then they said that I really do have to know, after I'd made such efforts, and then they, the whole committee of this memorial site, write that they regret that I have to read about it yet again. And yes, I carry on reading, and it says there that my father was taken from Dachau – how he was transported there I still don't know – I'll probably find that out later in the autumn or right now in the spring [2004] – anyway, whatever the case, this 'cargo' – he certainly wasn't the only one – was brought to Hartheim ...[32]
>
> And as I continued reading I read that my father was gassed there. And that he wasn't just murdered after a few days, but the date of arrival was destroyed. Yes, that just shows how that lot worked. Picture the scene. They took this man in a train, or a bus or or a lorry, probably with a number of other people – because they hadn't made a special effort for him – from Dachau to Austria, roughly two hundred kilometres, and gassed him that very same day – it's all noted down, the second, the minute, and I ask myself: How did his clothes get back again to Dachau, because the urn and clothing with the brown cardboard package, the box, came to us from Dachau? How they lied to us! How people were deceived ... Now we know how my father really died ... And he wasn't so very far away from us at all: because we were in the 16th district and they killed him here in Hartheim. Probably without even a glass of water.[33]

Ceija Stojka is trying to set the record straight, but has never become bitter about the past:

> Otherwise I couldn't have breathed. Otherwise I would have gone under. You can't counter hatred with hatred. I got rid of all that, the evil, and then chose the path of goodness ... I'm not even angry with the people who did evil things to us ... when all's said and done, they are human beings, and that's just what human beings are like. They're not all the same. Each person has five fingers and the five fingers are different.

> Have a different nature. But I'll never develop feelings of hatred.[34]

Poetry and its Reverberations

Although the catalogue of her art includes a few poems, the new volume of poetry *Meine Wahl zu schreiben – ich kann es nicht* (My Choice to Write – I Have None) is a ground-breaking work, combining her poetry (in German, even sometimes in Austrian dialect, and in some cases with a translation into the Romani language), with photographs, documents, paintings and drawings.

As a poet, Ceija Stojka does not set out to capture particular experiences. As a woman who did not attend school during her childhood because of National Socialist policies, she does not write in a particular literary tradition. Nor has she mastered the skill of word processing. The 2003 volume consists of work selected and edited by writer and publisher Gerald Kurdoðlu Nitsche. Ceija had noted her innermost feelings and responses on pieces of paper or in exercise books, often accompanied by sketches and drawings, spilling from the pen like the words spill from her mouth. The reproduction of the poems is as close to the original as possible, but spelling, punctuation and use of upper and lower case have been standardised in the editing process. The original manuscripts show drawings intertwined with the words, which would be difficult to reproduce in the printed version.

The themes of the groups of some 40 poems range from the historical, such as 'Auschwitz 1944',[35] or 'Welch ein Traum' (What a Dream), about the crematorium, searchlights, sirens and barracks,[36] to the soulful poem about a falling snowflake which evokes memories of her childhood in Vienna,[37] images of nature[38] and more personal expressions of fear, sadness and frustration.

The rhythm of the poems is dictated by the subject matter. There may, for example, be a question and answer, or statement and counter-statement. Where Ceija is celebrating life and nature, the rhythm is leisurely smooth, whereas when she is dealing with suffering there are more pauses and staccato sections for dramatic effect, as in this elegy to the dead, and her father in particular:

I
Ceija
say
Auschwitz lives
and breathes
even today in me
I still sense to this day
the suffering
Each blade of grass, each flower there
is the soul of a dead person
I have seen
everything is there again
everything is close again
Everywhere you sense
that the souls
accompany you
It is incomprehensible
that there were people
who could erect
such a site
of horror
Auschwitz was much worse
than today's wars
Auschwitz and its
equally bad siblings
wherever they all are and were
They brought with their
People-destroying gas factories
ash smoke urns
fire ash
ash in the urn
Who is really in the tin
Is it my father? (27.5.1955)[39]

Ceija Stojka's stark, staccato language attempts to express the horror of Auschwitz in poetry. James E. Young argues that the act of portraying violence may result in a loss of the violent quality in the narrative:

> For once written, events assume the mantle of coherence that narrative necessarily imposes on them, and the trauma of their unassailability is relieved.
>
> At the same time, however, there seems also to be a parallel and contradictory impulse on the part of writers to preserve in narrative the very discontinuity that lends events their violent character, the same discontinuity that is so effectively neutralized by its narrative rendering.[40]

The short fragmented form used by Ceija Stojka underlines the discontinuity, the break between her earlier childhood and its violent and abrupt end. It also serves to highlight the difficulty of living with fear:

> That which we seek
> is hard to find
> The fear
> we do not have to seek
> it is there [...][41]

It would, however, be wrong to see pessimism as the dominant emotion in her poems. In a celebration of family life she focuses on the unit of the family and its cohesion, looking to God for support as she muses on mortality:

> To my children grandchildren and great-great grandchildren
> and also to those to whom my mother gave birth
>
> I've lived my life with you and I was then myself just a child
> which is why I have also experienced everything with you
>
> We laughed with one another we cried with one another
> We also shared each pain with one another
> We shared each piece of bread with one another
> We are very strongly rooted together with one another
> We indeed really loved life with one another
> We made music and sang with one another
> [...]
> We lost many relatives to death with one another
> And yet we are and were happy with one another

> Think also always this and think that also with one another
> Whatever happens we love God and Mary with one another
> [...][42]

Art

In *Meine Wahl zu schreiben – ich kann es nicht*, editor and publisher Gerald Kurdoğlu Nitsche includes four pages of extracts from letters from school-pupils who met Ceija Stojka at an exhibition of her art in February 2002 in Landeck in Austria. They admire her work, her description of her childhood bravery, and her rejection of the concept of revenge, relating her images to their own world, in which xenophobic graffiti slogans stain walls and facades. They see her as a role model in the struggle for racial equality.

Just as the young people are uplifted by her work, so Ceija Stojka herself uses painting as a form of therapy, a way of expressing and transcending her 'stolen' childhood, a childhood characterised by fear, deprivation, pain and suffering. She had grown up in a world where brightly coloured carpets and fabrics abounded, and turned to art for solace, in an attempt to recapture moments of her pre-camp happy childhood and record her experiences for posterity, but also for herself:

> And every picture that you see there is not for any old person, but each one is for me. And this place, where this grass for example, is mixed by the wind with straw – yes, that's a place, somewhere I sat, and I have all of that inside me, as a travelling Romany child. And the horses and the caravan, the smell, and naturally the colours, which play an important role in our culture, the bright colours.[43]

The branch that accompanies her signature on each painting is her symbol and represents her salvation: 'Yes, if the branch hadn't existed, this little young tree in Bergen-Belsen, then I would probably have starved to death. But I ate the resin from the tree and its leaves. Yes, and I hug and kiss every tree, it's my friend ...'.[44] For her as a survivor, art offers a means of keeping in touch with those who have not been so fortunate:

> Just look, they're all in my home, the images of Auschwitz. You have to imagine that we had no pictures. When we experienced

3. Summer in the countryside.

4. Family faces (1997).

> the liberation there was nothing there. The little that we had they burnt. So when we were chauffeured away, and at the liberation, there was nothing there apart from the rags we were wearing.[45]

Ceija, like her brother Karl, is a self-taught artist. Both apply the paint with vigorous brush-strokes reminiscent of, but definitely not influenced by, the works of the German Expressionist painters, and use a bold, strong palette of vibrant, sparklingly vivid colours, as in her sunny image of a country stopping-place near a tree (see 3. Summer in the countryside).

Yet brightness of colour does not always equate with happiness, as in the tightly packed painting of family faces, many of which belong to relatives who perished in the concentration camps (see 4. Family faces).

In 'Sad earth' the dark shapes of fleeing birds, barracks, menacing rows of barbed wire, and the chimney stand out in stark contrast to the huddled forms of those assembled in the yard to be shot. Here, as in many of her brother Karl's works, the division of space into bands or blocks is almost reminiscent of the oriental carpets and rugs that would have been an important part of their everyday working lives after the end of the war (see 5. Sad earth).

The gaunt image of a man in a white, blue-white and creamy-white snowy landscape, to his right a dead bird spreadeagled across a stylised electric fence, is very slightly below the vanishing point of the painting, our gaze drawn to the two white globes of his eyes, with the pinpricks of black for pupils. The snow is lacerated again and again by the sharp lines of the barbed wire, and even the trees appear to conspire to take on oppressive swastika-like configurations, and to enclose and frame the seemingly naked man at the centre of the painting (see 6. Man in the snow).[46]

Even more bleak and desperate is the disturbing image of the inside of a bellowing Nazi's mouth. This is the most extreme example of the technique of 'disproportional representation',[47] whereby certain elements are no longer in proportion to others in order to draw the viewer's attention. The whites, browns and blacks of the face, with the shocking addition of blood red in the eyes, lips and tongue, contrast with the black of the cap, and its white swastika in the centre. The face almost resembles that of an animal, the teeth menacing and sharp, the eyelashes unnaturally spiky, and it appears

5. Sad earth.

6. Man in the snow (1998).

to be seen from below, from a small child's vantage point (see 7. Angry mouth).

Whereas the non-Romany representations of 'Gypsies' fluctuate between demonisation, romanticisation and exoticisation, in the same way that 'Orientalist' (to use Edward Said's terminology) images of Gypsies have been created over the centuries in literature and culture in general,[48] the Romany is always shown by Ceija Stojka as innocent, and the images of evil are those of the perpetrators, as in the black and white painting of a skull floating above a jagged-winged, black bird, with the words 'Verily we say unto you. We are not guilty' written in German (see 8. We are not guilty).

Ceija Stojka thus recaptures in art some of the moments of her early childhood. The peaceful, idyllic country scenes, the wagons, the horses, the kindness farmers show to the Romanies, all of this conveys an aura of tranquility and faith in humanity.

All the more powerful then are the dystopian images of brutality and inhumanity. In the scores of works piled in boxes in her Vienna apartment, most of which are in acrylic on card, there are countless images of barracks, of roll-call, of rows of people standing in the snow at the mercy of the SS with their machine guns, of inordinately large boots, mouths and noses of men looming high above the small child in a world out of control.

Ceija's Art and 'Holocaust Art'

There are almost no images of Romanies during the Nazi period, the exceptions being images produced by the German Expressionist artists Otto Pankok and Otto Mueller, and a series of less than a dozen official portraits of Romany children, commissioned by the Nazis in Auschwitz. Nor have any works of art created by Romanies in concentration camps survived. This is hardly surprising, since painting was not normally permitted, materials were in very short supply, there were no facilities for storing any works, and a large number of the few surviving works were by formally trained artists. There was no Romany tradition of going to art school, despite the Romanies' skill in applied arts such as coppersmithing or basket weaving.

The term 'Holocaust art' could be used to describe Ceija Stojka's artistic response to her experiences of the Nazi regime and its

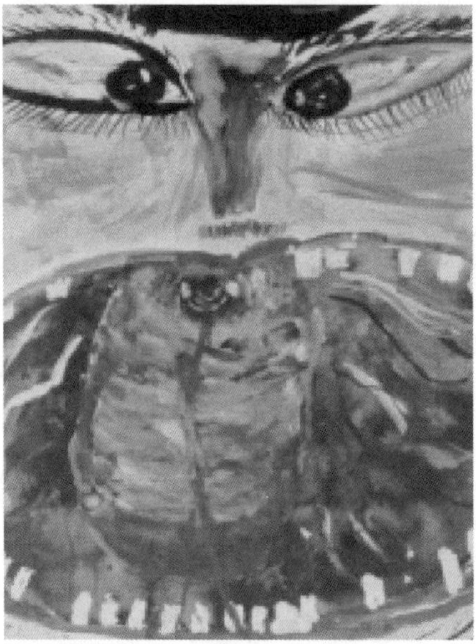

7. Angry mouth (1995).

8. We are not guilty.

aftermath, even though it was not created under duress during the Nazi regime.[49] Nevertheless there is a connection between the work produced by the Jewish refugees in Theresienstadt (some 60 kilometres north of Prague),[50] taught by Bauhaus artist Friedl Dicker-Brandeis,[51] and that of Ceija Stojka, in that Ceija also directs her anxieties into creative channels, and recalls images of childhood freedom as a way of surviving.[52]

Art was also a form of survival strategy for Berlin-born Jewish artist Charlotte Salomon (1917–43),[53] who was interned for several weeks in 1940 in Gurs camp in the Pyrenees and perished in Auschwitz. Her collection of over 1,300 gouaches, forming the autobiographical work *Life? or Theatre?* (1998), expresses in dramatic form many of the dilemmas she experienced. Whereas Salomon had an art training and painted her images during her confinement in the south of France, Ceija Stojka did not have the luxury of being able to paint during the Nazi period.

In 1945 Thomas Geve (1929–) committed his memories to paper in almost 80 drawings of the routine of the concentration camp. They are now preserved in Yad Vashem Museum in Israel.[54] Like Ceija, Thomas had no previous experience of painting or drawing, and no background of viewing art works in the original or as reproductions.

The term 'Holocaust art' thus embraces works produced under duress, whether in the concentration camps, ghettos or other sites, as well as those dealing with the experience but originating in the post-war period. Like the work of the children in Theresienstadt, Charlotte Salomon and Thomas Geve, Ceija Stojka's art captures the everyday experience as well as moments of great anguish and drama. It forms part of the collective history of the Romanies, and helps to bring the fate of this still marginalised minority into closer focus.

Conclusion

At the start of the twenty-first century Ceija Stojka is one of the very few Romany survivors to have depicted her experiences under the Nazis. She has not lost the *joie de vivre*, vitality and dynamism with which she promotes a greater understanding of the history of the genocide of the Romanies. Much remains to be learnt.

The discovery in January 2004 that her father had not died in Dachau, as the family had previously been led to believe, but in

Hartheim, much nearer to where she now lives, was a great shock for Ceija and her surviving siblings. It shows all too clearly how difficult it is to reconstruct a picture of the fate of the Romanies during the Nazi period, even when the sources are supposedly official.

The number of victims still able to bear witness to the crimes of the Nazis is diminishing rapidly. There is now a particularly urgent need to acknowledge the suffering of the Romany population, the majority of whom did not have any formal education, and were not in the habit of writing or painting. For these reasons it is all the more significant that Ceija Stojka has offered so many insights into her world and her experiences, and that out of the darkness have come hours of comfort for her in the creation of the works, and great inspiration for those who read her works and admire her paintings.

Despite all her suffering, Ceija Stojka remains optimistic. She continues to write and paint, to help future generations to avoid the mistakes of the past and to grow up with greater tolerance and understanding for minority groups in their midst. She highlights the uniqueness of each individual, whatever their racial origins. The reclaiming of her stolen childhood is both a painful and a joyous journey.

NOTES

Research for this article was supported by the Center for Advanced Holocaust Studies while I was a Charles H. Revson Foundation Fellow at the United States Holocaust Memorial Museum, Washington, DC in 2001. Thanks to all staff and Fellows for their insights. The research was also supported by Mary Immaculate College Research Seed Funding Scheme. Thanks also to Ceija Stojka for her generosity and helpfulness. She kindly agreed to be interviewed, and allowed me to photograph many of her paintings and drawings, and kindly gave permission for works to be reproduced here. All interviews were transcribed by Kirsten Guschal. Unless stated otherwise, the translations from the German are my own.

1. Extract from interviews that I conducted with Ceija Stojka, Vienna, 12 January 2004. To avoid any possible confusion with other members of her family, I refer to Ceija Stojka by her full name throughout the article, except when referring to Ceija as a child.
2. Ceija Stojka, *Wir leben im Verborgenen: Erinnerungen einer Rom-Zigeunerin*, ed. Karin Berger (Vienna: Picus, 1988).

3. All photographs by Susan Tebbutt. The paintings are in acrylic on board, and are reproduced here in black and white; the originals are strikingly vivid in their colour.
4. Ceija Stojka, *Reisende auf dieser Welt: Aus dem Leben einer Rom-Zigeunerin*, ed. Karin Berger (Vienna: Picus, 1992).
5. Researcher Karin Berger has published widely on the fate of women under National Socialism and the history of the Sinti and Roma. Since 1984 she has also been active as a filmmaker.
6. Ceija Stojka, *Gedichte (Romanes, Deutsch) und Bilder: Meine Wahl zu schreiben – ich kann es nicht; O fallo de isgiri – me tschischanaf les*, trans. from Romani into German by Ceija and Nuna Stojka (Landeck: Eye, 2003).
7. The main catalogue of her works is Ceija Stojka, *Bilder und Texte 1989–1995* (Vienna: n.p., 1995).
8. *Ceija Stojka*, dir. Karin Berger, Navigator Films, 1999, available from www.navigatorfilm.at.
9. One of the earliest studies was published in 1981 by Donald Kenrick and Grattan Puxon, and reissued as *Gypsies under the Swastika* (Hatfield: University of Hertfordshire Press, 1995). In chronological order, four of the key works on the Romanies and genocide are David M. Crowe and John Kolsti (eds.), *The Gypsies of Eastern Europe*, with an introduction by Ian Hancock (New York and London: M.E. Sharpe, 1991); Michael Zimmermann, *Rassenutopie und Genozid: Die nationalsozialistische 'Lösung der Zigeunerfrage'* (Hamburg: Christians, 1996); Wolfgang Wippermann, *'Wie die Zigeuner': Antisemitismus und Antiziganismus im Vergleich* (Berlin: Elefanten Press, 1997); Guenter Lewy, *The Nazi Persecution of the Gypsies* (Oxford, London and New York: Oxford University Press, 2000).
10. Alwin Meyer, *Die Kinder von Auschwitz* (Göttingen: Lamuv, 1995).
11. Edgar Bamberger and Annegret Ehmann (eds.), *Kinder und Jugendliche als Opfer des Holocaust* (Heidelberg: Dokumentations- und Kulturzentrum Deutscher Sinti und Roma, 1995). See also George Eisen, *Children and Play in the Holocaust: Games among the Shadows* (Amherst, MA: University of Massachusetts Press, 1988), for a study of play and the spirit of defiance and resistance. It contains no specific references to Romanies.
12. Otto Rosenberg, *A Gypsy in Auschwitz*, as told to Ulrich Enzenberger, trans. from German by Helmut Bögler (London: London House, 1999), first published in German as *Das Brennglas* (Frankfurt am Main: Eichborn, 1998).
13. For an overview of accounts by Romanies from Germany, Austria and Eastern Europe, see Susan Tebbutt (ed.), *Sinti and Roma: Gypsies in German-speaking Society and Literature* (New York and Oxford: Berghahn, 1998), pp.133–43.
14. Karl Stojka and Reinhard Pohanka, *Auf der ganzen Welt zu Hause: Das Leben und Wandern des Zigeuners Karl Stojka* (Vienna: Picus, 1994).
15. Karl Stojka, *Ein Kind in Birkenau* (Vienna: Eigendruck, 1995), *Gas*, 2nd edn. (Vienna: Eigendruck, 1998), and *Mein Name im Dritten Reich: Z 5742*, with some texts translated into English by Sonja Haderer-Stippel (Vienna: Eigendruck, 2000).
16. See Susan Tebbutt, '"My name in the Third Reich was Z: 5742": The Political Art of the Austrian Rom, Karl Stojka', in Thomas Acton (ed.), *Scholarship and the Gypsy struggle: Commitment in Romani Studies* (Hatfield: University of Hertfordshire Press, 2000), pp.69–80, for an analysis of Stojka's politicised artistic testimony.
17. Mongo Stojka, *Papierene Kinder: Glück, Zerstörung und Neubeginn einer Roma-Familie in Österreich* (Vienna: Molden, 2000).
18. See Homi K. Bhabha, *The Location of Culture* (London: Routledge, 1994).
19. See Susan Tebbutt, 'Marginalisation and Memories: Ceija Stojka's Autobiographical Writing', in Allyson Fiddler (ed.), *'Other' Austrians: Post-1945 Austrian Women's*

Writing (Berne: Peter Lang, 1998), pp.141–51.

20. This includes the interview with Ceija Stojka published in a volume of interviews with women who survived Ravensbrück concentration camp, Astrid Zach and Helga Amesberger, 'Ceija Stojka', in Helga Amesberger and Brigitte Halbmayr (eds.), *Vom Leben und Überleben – Wege nach Ravensbrück*, Vol.2, *Lebensgeschichten* (Vienna: Promedia, 2001), pp.216–22.
21. Ceija is also a talented musician, but this aspect of her artistic creativity falls outside the scope of the present article.
22. Ceija Stojka, *Wir leben im Verborgenen*, p.20.
23. Obviously any attempt to render dialect in the form of any dialect of English (such as Scottish, Yorkshire or Cockney) would be extremely misleading, and I have thus translated all expressions into Standard English. The poems are aligned or justified according to how they appear in the volume.
24. Ceija Stojka, *Wir leben im Verborgenen*, p.21.
25. Ibid., p.31.
26. Ibid., p.56.
27. Ibid., p.57.
28. Ceija Stojka, *Reisende auf dieser Welt*, p.105.
29. The continuity of anti-Gypsyism was not only manifest in incidents affecting individual Romanies, but was more widespread in academic, legal and professional circles, as Sybil Milton argues in 'Persecuting the Survivors: The Continuity of "Anti-Gypsyism" in Postwar Germany and Austria', in Susan Tebbutt (ed.), *Sinti and Roma: Gypsies in German-Speaking Society and Literature* (New York and Oxford: Berghahn, 1998), pp.35–47.
30. Ceija Stojka, *Wir leben im Verborgenen*, p.104.
31. Ibid., p.149.
32. The medieval Hartheim Palace in Austria (now a Memorial Site) served under the Nazis as a centre for 'euthanasia' of over 18,000 physically and mentally disabled, who were killed by gassing and lethal injection. The palace was also used from 1941 to 1945 as an extermination centre for inmates from the nearby Mauthausen concentration camp.
33. Interview with Ceija Stojka, Vienna, 12 January 2004.
34. Ibid.
35. Ceija Stojka, *Gedichte (Romanes, Deutsch) und Bilder*, pp.16–17.
36. Ibid., p.18.
37. Ibid., p.48.
38. 'Wenn die Gräser', Ceija Stojka, *Gedichte (Romanes, Deutsch) und Bilder*, p.29, is, for example, about grass dancing in the wind, daisies, the dew, sun and summer warmth.
39. Ceija Stojka, *Gedichte (Romanes, Deutsch) und Bilder*, p.24. The poem is printed with right-justification.
40. James E. Young, *Writing and Rewriting the Holocaust: Narrative and the Consequences of Interpretation* (Bloomington and Indianapolis: Indiana University Press, 1990), p.16.
41. Ceija Stojka, *Gedichte (Romanes, deutsch) und Bilder*, p.20.
42. Ibid., p.62.
43. Interview with Ceija Stojka, Vienna, 16 January 2004.
44. Interview with Ceija Stojka, Vienna, 12 January 2004.
45. Interview with Ceija Stojka, Vienna, 16 January 2004.
46. Compare these with the works of Karl Stojka, *Gas* (Vienna: Eigenverlag, 1996). His paintings are often divided into broad horizontal bands by rows of barbed wire, which may appear to be twisted into a swastika-like shape.

47. See Susan Tebbutt, 'Disproportional Representation: Romanies and European Art', in N. Saul and S. Tebbutt (eds.), *The Role of the Romanies: Images and Self-Images of 'Gypsies' in European Culture* (Liverpool: Liverpool University Press, 2004), pp.159–77.
48. See Susan Tebbutt, 'Sinti und Roma: Antiziganismus und Orientalismus', in Jim Jordan and Peter Barker (eds.), *Migrants in German-Speaking Countries: Aspects of Social and Cultural Experience*, Modern German Studies, vol.2 (London: CILT, 2000), pp.156–82.
49. See Sybil Milton, 'Culture under Duress: Art and the Holocaust', in F.C. Decoste and Bernard Schwartz (eds.), *The Holocaust's Ghost: Writings on Art, Politics, Law and Education* (Edmonton and Alberta: University of Alberta Press, 2000), pp.84–96. In the same volume, Stephen C. Feinstein, 'Art after Auschwitz: Jozef Szajna's "Theatre of Panic"', pp.109–23, deals with survivors who depicted their story after 1945, focusing on the work of a Jewish survivor, Samuel Bak, and the traditional and installation art of a Polish political prisoner, Josef Szajna. Only one sentence is devoted to Romanies. Karl Stojka is described as 'perhaps the only member of the Sinti-Gypsy survivor group who has chosen to paint his experiences'.
50. Of the 12,000 children under 18 deported from Theresienstadt to Auschwitz, only about 1,560 aged 15 or below survived at liberation. See Sybil Milton, 'Art in the Context of Theresienstadt', in Anne Dutlinger (ed.), *Art, Music and Education as Strategies for Survival: Theresienstadt 1941–45* (New York and London: Herodias, 2001), p.26.
51. See also Helga Weissová, *Zeichne, was Du siehst: Zeichnungen eines Kindes aus Theresienstadt/Terezín* (Göttingen: Wallstein, 1998), p.155; and Hana Volavková (ed.), *'I never saw another butterfly': Children's Drawings and Poems from Terezin Concentration Camp 1942–1944*, expanded 2nd edn. by United States Holocaust Memorial Museum, foreword by Chaim Potok and afterword by Vaclav Havel (New York: Schocken, 1993).
52. See Nelly Toll, *When Memory Speaks: The Holocaust in Art* (Westport, CT and London: Praeger, 1998), p.40. Theresienstadt was presented to the outside world as a model of cultural life. Toll includes both the work of survivors and that of artists whose work is based on research into the period. Romanies are conspicuous by their absence from the volume.
53. See Charlotte Salomon, *Life? or Theatre?*, with Introduction by Judith C.E. Belinfante, Christine Fischer-Defoy, Ad Petersen and Norman Rosenthal, trans. Leila Vennewitz (Zolle, Waanders and London: Royal Academy of Art, 1998). Charlotte was 25 when she completed the paintings, which presented an artistic translation of her own life. Salomon's testimony is reviewed by Mary Felstiner in 'Charlotte Salomon's Inward-Turning Testimony', in Decoste and Schwartz (eds.), *The Holocaust's Ghost*, pp.55–64.
54. See Thomas Geve, *Es gibt hier keine Kinder – Auschwitz, Groß-Rosen, Buchenwald: Zeichnungen eines kindlichen Historikers* [There are no Children Here – Auschwitz, Groß-Rosen, Buchenwald: Drawings of a Child Historian] (Wallstein: Göttingen, 1997); see also Nicholas Stargardt's essay in this volume, 'Drawing the Holocaust in 1945', pp. 25–37.

Between Adult Narrator and Narrated Child: Autobiographical Writing by Former Members of the *Kindertransporte*

ANDREA HAMMEL

In a review of a recent volume focusing on the *Kindertransporte* to Britain entitled *Die Kindertransporte 1938/9: Rettung und Integration*,[1] Birgit Aschmann writes about the structural problem 'that studies of the persecution of Jews either descend into a sterile history of institutions or get lost in the attempt to follow individual lives'.[2] The analysis of autobiographical texts by former members of the *Kindertransporte* is faced with a similar problem. Does a study of these texts have to exclude the history of the rescue efforts for Jewish children from Germany in the late 1930s and any general conclusions to be able to do justice to the individuality of the life story? Does an examination of these autobiographies have to leave aside autobiographical theory because of the personal and testimonial nature of the texts? Or is it actually the tension between the history of institutions and the story of the individual, between literary theory and personal writing, where the meaning of the autobiographical text is situated? The classification of the autobiographical text as located between history and literature has lead to a dichotomisation of the interpretations. Within historical studies autobiographical texts have been embraced as a resource deemed especially suited to breaking up the 'grand narrative' theory of history. Within literary studies, on the other hand, the autobiographical discourse as such is the subject. This essay will argue that the different approaches complement each other and I will attempt to show that the examination of these autobiographical texts can make a contribution to interdisciplinary research.

Following a brief survey of the terminology relating to the genre of autobiography and memoir, and a discussion of the cultural concept of memory, I will investigate the cultural parameter of *Kindertransport* narrative. I intend to demonstrate that the search for identity for both the reader and the writer is located in the tension between the text as resource and as autobiographical discourse. I will also show that the analysis of these autobiographical narratives could have an impact on debates about the portrayal of the childhood self in life writing.

The aforementioned dichotomy between the critical discourse of history and literature influences the genre definition of autobiography and memoir on a fundamental level. Helen Buss argues that 'traditional autobiography makes the individual life central, while memoirs tend to focus on the times in which the life is lived and the significant others of the memoirist's world'.[3] Memoirs as the genre that personalises history and historicises the personal is thus, so one could argue, the proper categorisation for the narratives at the heart of this essay as they focus on a specific historical phenomenon, the *Kindertransporte* to Britain, 1938–39, with each being constructed as a personal story of a participant. Buss furthermore points out that there is a 'close connection between the act of testifying and the memoir form' and refers to accounts of the Holocaust such as Eli Wiesel's *All Rivers Run to the Sea: A Memoir*.[4]

However, historians of autobiography have interpreted the difference between autobiography and memoir in terms of a hierarchy: Laura Marcus refers to Georg Misch and his *Geschichte der Autobiographie* (published 1907) for a definition of the distinction between memoir and autobiography. Misch, who incidentally was later in life also a German refugee in Britain, argues that the memoir 'has come to possess more superficial associations as a "merely" historical resource, without literary pretensions or the securing of the identity of the subject and the object, which is the central purpose and interest of autobiography'.[5] Misch also reserves a more passive role for the memoir writer, who observes the events he or she writes about, whereas the author of an autobiography is obviously central to the life story narrated, thus achieving subject-object unity to a greater degree.[6] Misch goes on to argue that 'the man who sets out to write the story of his own life has it in view as a whole, with unity and direction and significance of its own'.[7] This is, of course, not only contentious because of the male-centredness of Misch's argument, but it does not seem to fit narratives, which are based on rupture and contingency as most of those written by former members of the *Kindertransporte* clearly are.

But it is not only the claim of a unified self as such that is a problematic concept. To express this unified self, demarcation between it and others is necessary. For Misch self-awareness and self-assertion seem to be synonymous: 'To stand as an I, or, more exactly, as an "I" saying person, over against other persons and living beings and the things that live around us implies that we are aware of our independent existence ... Self-awareness gives us the feeling that the impetus of life is sort of emanating from ourselves'.[8] Misch therefore assumes for the author of an autobiography a position of power; the author is someone who can assert 'the centrality of self by viewing the world as an "emanation" from the self'.[9]

This unified stable self that Misch imagined in the early 1900s is seen as problematic today. Critics of the late twentieth century see a fragmented self that is engaged in a continuous process of evolvement. This explains, on the one hand, why autobiographies by former members of the *Kindertransporte* are often seen only in terms of memoir writing and therefore analysed as historical resource, which in turn diminishes their value in the eyes of those who still adhere to a hierarchical difference between memoirs and autobiographies.

Memory, too, has become a much debated category and it is now acknowledged that, as Ann Gray puts it, 'memory is not simply there to be re-presented in one's reflection on life, but something which must be selected, constructed and told'.[10] The social and cultural dimension of memory is the focus. 'Narratives of memory are understood to be expressed within and through a framework in which certain narratives become possible'.[11]

Caroline Steedman examined how self-narration became a 'taught and learned activity' influenced, for example, by creative writing teaching practices.[12] However, this is only the most obvious form of shaping autobiographical narratives. For former members of the *Kindertransporte*, reading other representations of the *Kindertransporte*, the public interest in such accounts, and the realisation that the *Kindertransporte* were not an individual, but a shared experience, shaped their impetus to write and the form of their narratives.

If we accept that the route from memory to autobiographical narrative is complex, we need to ask questions about truth and authenticity. The former members of the *Kindertransporte* are aware of these issues, as one of them has pointed out in a letter to the author of this essay: 'my writings may present a slightly different point of view. For one I have the impression that the *Kindertransport* literature emphasizes too much the young children who lost their German language and culture'.[13] The letter is at pains to point out differences between accounts without wanting to question the validity of other accounts.

Some of these differences relate to the time in which the autobiographical texts were written; the texts under consideration here were published between 1983 and 2001. They reflect to some extent the public perception of the history of National Socialism and refugees coming to Britain as well as the changing acknowledgement of the *Kindertransport* experience. For example, most *Kindertransport* narratives are chronologically structured. They start with the family background of the biological parents, reaching back to the time before the authors were born, and recount their early lives in Germany and Austria. Most of the texts briefly describe life before and under Nazi persecution and relate the parents' decision to send their children to safety in the United Kingdom. This structure conforms to narrative conventions. But the length of the narrative devoted to this introductory part varies: Hannele Zürndorfer dedicates a longer section of her report to life under the Nazi regime. Her autobiography, entitled *The Ninth of November* – a significant title because, unlike others, it does not refer to the *Kindertransporte* – was published in 1983 and has a different focus. She obviously felt the need to explain her early life in Germany in greater detail and thus gives the reader a better idea of what her family had to endure under National Socialism. Autobiographies written and published later presuppose more knowledge of the history of Jewish persecution in Germany in the 1930s and place greater emphasis on describing life in Britain. This is significant as, for a long time, *Kindertransport* children had been regarded as 'those to whom nothing happened at all', meaning that the overwhelming majority had not been incarcerated in a concentration camp.[14] As most of them were only little when arriving in Britain, they were, moreover, deemed too young to remember any trauma or, at least, it was considered easier for them to integrate into a new society.[15] Of course, trauma experts have since revised these somewhat naïve assumptions.[16] Autobiographical texts with differing emphases might be seen as supporting the view that child refugees are unreliable witnesses. I am, however, arguing that Hannele Zürndorfer's text should not be considered any less or more authentic than others written later. The memory researcher and Nobel laureate Eric Kandel, who as a child emigrated from Vienna to the US, coined the term 'ripened memories' in a recent interview in the German magazine *Der Spiegel*, pointing to a lifelong interaction between experiences and memory.[17] It is thus a matter for both the researcher and the reader 'to untangle the relationships between discourses and experiences by exploring the ways in which subjects mediated and transformed discourses in specific historical settings'.[18] It is also important to note the differences between texts written for an English-speaking and for a German-speaking readership.[19]

Using *Kindertransport* narratives as a resource can give the researcher useful information about many issues relating to the children's experiences, including their adaptation to different circumstances, their coping with trauma and their identity formation. One such issue is language acquisition. It is hardly surprising that all *Kindertransport* autobiographies I have examined so far refer to initial difficulties with the English language. Hannele Zürndorfer in *The Ninth of November* focuses on the painful beginning of an ultimately successful process of language acquisition. On her first days at school she remembers feeling 'like being deaf-mute in a busy crowd'.[20] Martha Blend in *A Child Alone* describes her frustration at being 'cut off from the mainstream of events'.[21] Her terminology is illuminating, as her placement, an immigrant East European Jewish family in the East End of London, can also be seen as outside the mainstream of British society. Blend communicates with her foster parents in German, of which they have a basic knowledge. Moreover, the affinity between spoken German and Yiddish aids communication with her East End neighbours. But at school she has to cope with a whole new frame of reference on her own. As immigrants, her foster parents cannot help her understand the idiosyncratic usage of English names and terms. In her text Blend uses an amusing anecdote to illustrate this:

> 'What's father temsis?' I asked, one day after a singing lesson.
> 'Father temsis? No such ting', replied my uncle.
> 'Yes, there is!' I insisted. 'We sang it today: old father temsis rolling along down to the mighty sea.' Bewilderment all round. Another time Werner, the young man from Berlin, who was still staying with us and was learning the tailoring trade, asked for a 'simble' – as he pronounced in his German accent. My uncle smiled indulgently. 'Not "simble" – "timble"', he corrected. (The object in question was, of course, a thimble, the English 'th' sound eluding both of them.)[22]

However, it is not the anecdote as such which is the most interesting aspect of this narrative. Treated as a social historical resource the passage confirms information found in other narratives by former child refugees. This early stage of acculturation marked by the inability to communicate in the new language has become part of the common discourse in child refugee narratives, especially with reference to the situation at school. It figures even in fictional accounts, as in Judith Kerr's *When Hitler Stole Pink Rabbit*, where the main character Anna is said to have made 142 mistakes in the first dictation in her new French school. What all these stories share is the obvious discrepancy between the initial lack of language skills and the successful command of it as demonstrated by the report. While this constructs the 'success story' discourse of the refugee narrative, in Kerr's book it is also part of the 'adventure story' discourse characteristic of children's literature, where the child frustrates the adult's expectation of conforming to a certain norm. Language acquisition is thus a good example of how the *Kindertransport* text can serve both as historical resource and as literary discourse. Indeed, analysis of the literary discourse here helps the reader understand the historical situation.

Although we expect different standards of truth and authenticity in an autobiographical text such as Martha Blend's *A Child Alone*, in my opinion it is its literary discourse which holds our interest. Blend's text is an important resource for information on a *Kindertransport* child, who was placed in a foster family with an ethnic, linguistic, class background and educational aspirations different from that of her biological family. As literary discourse, *A Child Alone* provides us with an opportunity to investigate further the success story discourse in a refugee autobiography. Yet it is precisely the tension between these two discourses that allows the adult writer to preserve the awkward singularity of the child who has successfully overcome her difficulties and is now an educator herself. The tension between resource and discourse gives us the opportunity to investigate the narratives within the parameters of the success story discourse of the immigrant.

As per definition, 'the child' is at the heart of *Kindertransport* narratives. It is also an intrinsic part of autobiographical writing. If we consider that psychoanalysis interprets the child as the adult's ontological origin and that the child is figured as that which comes before the subject, the discussion needs to encompass the subject–object dichotomy. Jo-Ann Wallace argues that the 'child' 'destabilizes many of the premises of theories of the agential subject'.[23] In *Kindertransport* narratives the representation of the agential subject is especially interesting. Vera Gissing in *Pearls of Childhood* presents the child Vera as very determined, especially in view of her Czech identity. Gissing describes herself as having been in the enviable position of having two foster families, the Rainfords and, after evacuation from Liverpool to Stockport, Aunt Margery, both of which looked after her well and are described as loving and caring. When her initial foster family moves nearer to Stockport, she is faced with the dilemma of whether to move back with the Rainfords or to stay with her evacuation host mother, Aunt Margery. A compromise is found and she relates her happiness about the fact that she commutes between the two families: 'I never moved in and I never moved out!'[24] Nevertheless she feels the pressing need to be with other Czech refugee children. In 1941 she leaves both her host families to attend a Czech boarding school in Hinton Hall, near Whitchurch in Shropshire. She describes her overwhelming sense of belonging: 'I had arrived, I felt at ease and at home'.[25]

Quite differently, Martha Blend constructs the child subject of her text as someone to whom things happen and who suffers from the lack of explanations given: one of the teachers at her grammar school suggests she should take up German as a third 'foreign language'. In retrospect the narrator reflects about the lack of explanation for the decisions she received from those adults in charge of the child. This kind of comment surfaces repeatedly in the narrative:

> It was typical of those times that nobody made any attempt to explain the reasoning behind this imaginative idea of my teachers, but it enabled me later to join up some fragments of my broken links with the past.[26]

Charles Leigh expresses a similar helplessness, when faced with his foster parents' decisions. He shows that the procedure of evacuation was a convenient moment for his first foster family to get rid of him:

> Before leaving me that day, Mr. Burns told me, that it wasn't possible for him and his wife to take me back to their home in Frognal, but that I should keep in touch by writing to them. The news came as a bit of a shock to me, and I had this terrible feeling of abandonment ... It was rather presumptuous of them to think that someone else was prepared to take over the burden of looking after me, especially as they didn't get full payment for my upkeep. I was like an article of goods that was changing hands.[27]

While Martha has learnt to see the positive that has come of past hurt, Charles dwells on the helplessness of the pre-agential child and therefore is still bitter about his treatment.

Claudia Castaneda criticises the attitude of cultural studies researchers towards 'the child': 'Rather than figuring a particular child or groups of children in historically and culturally (or socially) specific webs of relations, "the child" all too often appears in much more generic forms'.[28] Because the child is categorised as an adult's 'Other', its individuality is often not fully investigated. Here *Kindertransport* narratives provide an obvious source for children to be investigated in their historically and culturally specific relations. Their unaccompanied move from one country to another is a *caesura*, which can serve as a focus for researchers. This research can thus challenge what Teresa de Lauretis calls 'fantasies of origin', that is, 'cultural myths that have a powerful hold on subjectivity'.[29] During a recent research project on the subject conducted at the Centre for German-Jewish Studies at Sussex University,[30] it has become obvious that many former members of the *Kindertransporte* link their failures as adults causally with their early childhood experiences. One interviewee, for example, interprets her lack of success in trying to become a published author as a direct consequence of her *Kindertransport* experience. While someone with a more 'normal' life story might either see the reason for this failure in the lack of talent or blame the publishers, narrators of the *Kindertranport* texts more than likely attribute such experience to the rupture in their biographies. Thus they view their later lives as a kind of inescapable fate, which was largely determined by their earlier experiences.

Both Vera Gissing and Martha Blend end their autobiographical narratives with the portrayal of reunions, Gissing with a reunion weekend at the former Czech school and Blend with the first *Kindertransport* reunion organised by Bertha Leverton in London in June 1989. Group identity thus provides a powerful impetus for the narratives. These endings contrast with such titles as Martha Blend's *A Child Alone*, and *I Came Alone: The Stories of the Kindertransports*, edited by Bertha Leverton and Shmuel Lowensohn.[31] Autobiographical narratives by former *Kindertransport* children provide multiple questions regarding the view that to express a unified self, separation from others is deemed necessary. Indeed, neither the model of the unified self nor that of multiple fragmentations is entirely convincing. Although the biographies of former members of the *Kindertransporte* provide enough examples of change and rupture, the narratives also tell of successful integration and linking together. It seems clear that the emerging group identity of former *Kindertransport* children enabled individuals to narrate their childhood. Moreover, the shared experience grants the authors a position of power, which is in part provided by the variations in their experiences and in part by the similarities. This tension has been recognised in the autobiographical narrations of other marginal groups, which are said to portray a 'stereotyping by categorisation and what Trinh T Minh Ha has called "planned authenticity", in which a group may be required to accentuate its difference as defined by a dominant culture'.[32] It is this tension between the difference and sameness that is most illuminating, also when we compare the experience of the former *Kindertransport* children with those living in hiding. Moreover, both share certain life experiences with children who grow up in 'normal' circumstances; puberty is a case in point. In 1997 Katherine Viner, on the occasion of the publication of the uncut version of the *Diary of Anne Frank*, compared her own teenage diary, written in Yorkshire in the 1980s, with that of Anne Frank written in 1940s Amsterdam. She was surprised at the striking similarities between her own and Anne Frank's worries: 'What this uncut work reveals is that, though hidden away and fearful of discovery by the Nazis, Anne Frank went through the same angst as all teenage girls'.[33] When Martha Blend focuses on her puberty, her conflicts with her parents show this tension:

> Having two sets of parents so different from each other, and being brought up in so many contradictory cultures made life extremely difficult for me ... From remarks she let drop, I think my aunt [her foster mother] had a rosy picture of motherhood with an obedient child as a perpetual companion – a cross between Lord Fauntleroy and Goody Two Shoes. Such unrealistic expectations were doomed to be disappointed. Her narrow and dogmatic ideas often clashed with mine ... [The arguments] gave me the chance to pour out words and phrases with an eloquence my aunt could not match ... When she was thoroughly wound up, she would shout at me: 'You wouldn't do this, if I were your real mother!' I could find no answer to this unfair charge. This would occasionally be followed by the threat 'I'll report you to Bloomsbury House!'[34]

Using Blend's text as a resource we can see the 'normality' of her teenage arguments with her foster mother. 'You wouldn't do this, if I were your real mother!' elicits the spontaneous reaction 'Oh, yes, she would'. At the same time the reader is aware of the consequences for the child had the aunt's threat been realised.

As literary critics we can appreciate Blend's acculturation by following her discourse rich in references to British culture such as *Little Lord Fauntleroy*, a classic children's book by Frances Hodgson Burnett, and *The History of Goody Two-Shoes*, one of the earliest London children's stories, published in 1765 by John Newbery.[35] While Blend's story dwells on the culturally and historically specific aspect of her upbringing, that is, that she was a foster child who came from another country on a *Kindertransport* at the same time she asserts her Britishness with references to well-known children's literature.

The attempt by former *Kindertransport* children to locate their selfs in relation to cultural meta-narratives is a powerful means that allows the texts to transcend their narrow definition as mere historical resource. The autobiographical character of the texts allows us to make inferences about the social history of the

Kindertransport phenomena. Indeed, the study of *Kindertransport* narratives highlights the importance of historically and culturally specific circumstances in which children grow up, and that these need to be considered when talking about narratives of childhood in more generic terms. Studying autobiographical texts by former members of the *Kindertransporte* also makes clear how the fragmentation of their childhood influences the narration of the rest of their life story. Thus we must react cautiously to postmodern attempts of recent decades, which by celebrating the fragmented self seem to deny autobiographical authors such as the ones discussed in this essay the right to see the changes and ruptures in their lives as traumatic. Either way, this shows that *Kindertransport* narratives can provide us with examples of how to break up the dichotomy between literary discourse and social historical resource and demand an investigation of their interrelationship.

NOTES

1. Wolfgang Benz, Claudia Curio and Andrea Hammel (eds.), *Die Kindertransporte 1938/9: Rettung und Integration* (Frankfurt: Fischer Taschenbuch, 2003).
2. '*daß Studien zur Judenverfolgung entweder zur nüchternen Institutionengeschichte gerinnen ... oder sich im Nachvollzug individueller Lebenswege zerfasern*'. Birgit Aschmann, 'Hübsch und Blond', *Frankfurter Allgemeine Zeitung*, No.258, 6 November 2003, p.8.
3. Helen M. Buss, 'Memoirs', in Margaretta Jolly (ed.), *Encyclopedia of Life Writing*, Vol.2 (London: Fitzroy and Dearborn, 2001), p.595.
4. Ibid., p.596.
5. Laura Marcus, *Auto/Biographical Discourses: Theory, Criticism, Practice* (Manchester: Manchester University Press, 1994), p.149.
6. Ibid., p.149.
7. Ibid., p.150.
8. Ibid., p.151.
9. Ibid.
10. Ann Gray, *Research Practice for Cultural Studies: Ethnographic Methods and Lived Cultures* (London: Sage, 2003), p.123.
11. Ibid., p.123.
12. Carolyn Steedman, 'Writing the Self: The End of the Scholarship Girl', in Jim McGuigan (ed.), *Cultural Methodologies* (London: Sage, 1997), pp.109–10.
13. Helmut Kallmann in a letter to Andrea Hammel, 10 May 2003, Archive of the Centre for German-Jewish Studies, University of Sussex.
14. The Database of British Archival Resources Relating to German-Speaking Refugees, 1933–1950 (BARGE), which is funded by the AHRB and currently being compiled at the Centre for German-Jewish Studies, University of Sussex, so far contains material relating to three such individuals who were incarcerated in camps in the 1930s, consequently released and came on a *Kindertransport*.

15. Dorit Bader Whiteman, *The Uprooted: A Hitler Legacy* (New York and London: Plenum Press, 1993), esp. pp.1–10.
16. For a more detailed discussion of this subject, see Ruth Barnett, 'Familiengedächtnis: Erste und zweite Generation in der therapeutischen Praxis', in Benz, Curio and Hammel (eds.), *Die Kindertransporte 1938/9*, pp.156–70.
17. Eric Kandel, '"Wissen, wie der Geist funktioniert", Interview mit Johann Grolle und Gerhard Traufetter', *Der Spiegel*, No.18, 28 April 2003, p.152.
18. Kathleen Canning, quoted in Gray, *Research Practice for Cultural Studies*, p.116.
19. For a more detailed discussion of this difference, see Andrea Hammel, 'The Destabilisation of Personal Histories: Rewriting and Translating Autobiographical Texts by German-Jewish Survivors', in Lucia Boldrini and Peter Davies (eds.), *Comparative Critical Studies. Autobiografictions: Comparatists' Essays*, Vol.1, No.3 (Edinburgh: Edinburgh University Press, 2004), pp.95–308.
20. Hannele Zürndorfer, *The Ninth of November* (London: Quartet Books, 1983), p.89.
21. Martha Blend, *A Child Alone* (London: Vallentine Mitchell, 2001), p.58.
22. Ibid., p.61.
23. Jo-Ann Wallace, 'Technologies of the Child: Towards a Theory of the Child Subject', *Textual Practices*, Vol.9 (Summer 1995), p.295.
24. Vera Gissing, *Pearls of Childhood: A Poignant True Wartime Story of a Girl Growing up in an Adopted Land* (London: Robson Books, 1988), p.75.
25. Ibid., p.86.
26. Blend, *A Child Alone*, p.105.
27. Charles Leigh, 'The Autobiography of a Jewish Refugee', unpublished manuscript, Centre for German-Jewish Studies, University of Sussex, p.43.
28. Claudia Castaneda, 'The Child as Feminist Figuration: Towards a Politics of Privilege', *Feminist Theory*, Vol.2, No.1 (2001), p.31.
29. Teresa de Lauretis, quoted in Castaneda, 'The Child as Feminist Figuration', p.41.
30. Ten oral history interviews were conducted by Edward Timms and Andrea Hammel at the Centre for German-Jewish Studies, University of Sussex, between October 2003 and December 2004 with ten former members of the *Kindertransporte* who have written autobiographical texts. This research was part of a British Academy funded project on 'The "Kindertransport" Children: Identity, Adaptation and Trauma'.
31. Berta Leverton and Shmuel Lowensohn (eds.), *I Came Alone: Stories of the Kindertransports* (Sussex: Book Guild, 1990).
32. Marcus, *Auto/Biographical Discourses*, p.223.
33. Katherine Viner, 'Dear Diary', *Guardian*, 21 January 1997.
34. Blend, *A Child Alone*, pp.120–1.
35. It comes from the title of a rather moralistic nursery tale called *The History of Goody Two-Shoes*, which is thought to have been written by Oliver Goldsmith. Goody owned only one shoe. When she was given a pair of them, she was so pleased that she showed them to everybody, saying 'Two shoes'. The phrase now refers to a self-righteous, smugly virtuous person.

Between Persecution and Complicity: The Life Story of a Former 'Jewish *Mischling*'[1]

CATHY S. GELBIN

From 1995 to 1998, the Moses Mendelssohn Centre for European-Jewish Studies at Germany's Potsdam University interviewed more than 70 survivors of the *Shoah* living in Berlin and Brandenburg. More than a third of those interviewed by myself and others for the 'Archive of Memory' had one non-Jewish parent and were persecuted as 'first-degree *Mischlinge*' (lit. mongrels) during the Nazi period. The high level of participation of this group in our project was remarkable as many had maintained their survival strategy during the Nazi period and remained silent after the war had ended.[2] Their emerging stories suggest their increasing self-awareness as survivors in old age,[3] facilitated by the growing societal recognition of their particular history of persecution[4] at a time when narratives by other marginalised groups of survivors, such as child survivors, Roma and gay men, finally reached the public.

Gabriele Rosenthal, an eminent voice in the developing field of Biography Studies in Germany, has argued that biographical interviews indicate the available interpretative patterns both for constructing social reality at the time of the biographical experience and at the time of the narration.[5] Rosenthal's interest in the correlation between socio-political processes and individual patterns of coping with biographical experience transcends the focus on trauma in the works of Shoshanah Felman, Lawrence Langer and others working in the Anglo-American context,[6] and offers an appropriate tool for exploring the personal narratives of former '*Mischlinge*' beyond the aspect of victimisation. Through the ambiguities and contradictions within the life story of Ralf G, my article explores the under-researched plight of '*Mischlinge*' in Nazi Germany, the impact of persecution on the identity formation of this group and the ways in which wartime and post-war discourses affected the biographical narratives of individuals persecuted in this way.

Nineteenth-century racial theorists first applied the term '*Mischling*', which will be used in the following study, to human beings. The official jargon of the Nazi regime adopted this term as well as its negative connotation of racial impurity, and physical and mental degeneracy.[7] My use of this concept does not attempt to lend it renewed credibility, but rather to expose its racist implications and those of similar terms. As supposedly alternative designations such as 'half-Jew' or 'of partial Jewish descent' have the same racist overtones of racial impurity and inauthentic identity, the term '*Mischling*' serves me to explore the construct of the 'mixed-race Jew' in its historical and political context.

For want of a better word, many interviewees participating in the 'Archive of Memory' recurred to this term to describe their specific ostracism during the Nazi period. The Nazis' seizure of power constituted a radical rupture in the fully assimilated lifestyles of most adults from intermarried Christian-Jewish families who often felt little or no ties to Judaism. The vast majority of children from such unions were baptised Protestants, or in some cases Catholics, and only a few were affiliated with Judaism. The Nazis' racial laws classified the latter group as *Geltungsjuden* (those 'deemed Jews') rather than '*Mischlinge*' and equated them legally with the persecuted Jews. In contrast to Jews, '*Mischlinge*' did not form a historical collective with a positive self-definition prior to Nazi persecution. The Nineteenth-century biologistic construct of the 'Jewish *Mischling*' emerged as a socially defined term with the 1935 Nuremberg Laws. Robert Weltsch's famous exclamation to the persecuted Jews, 'wear the Yellow Badge with pride',[8] that is, to assert proudly their Jewishness through the symbol of ostracism, thus could not likewise apply to those persecuted as '*Mischlinge*'.

From Racial Theory to Nazi Politics

From early 1933 until the autumn of 1935, the Nazi legislation had distinguished between 'Aryans' and 'non-Aryans', and included those with at least one Jewish grandparent into the category of 'non-Aryans'. Presumably for political reasons – such as the Japanese allies' protest against the term 'non-Aryan' – the Nazi regime revised the initial laws. The Nuremberg Laws and the new *Reich* Citizenship Law of 1935 forbade marriage and extramarital relationships between 'Jews' and 'nationals of German or kindred blood', and outlined four 'racial' categories with varying legal positions. '*Deutschblütige*' ('of German blood') were defined as having four grandparents of 'German or kindred blood'. The 'Jewish' category included those descending from three or more grandparents of 'fully Jewish race', those that had 'two fully Jewish grandparents' and that were affiliated with Judaism or had married Jews, and all extramarital children born to Jews after 31 June 1936. All other German nationals with 'two fully Jewish' grandparents were regarded 'first-degree *Mischlinge*' and those with one 'fully Jewish' grandparent 'second-degree *Mischlinge*'.[9] The grandparents' affiliation with Judaism served as a proof of their descent, a religious definition that undermined the very notion of race.[10]

According to a commentary made by Hans Globke and Wilhelm Stuckart, both high-ranking officials in the *Reich* ministry of the interior,

> the intermingling of German and Jewish blood only transmitted the tension into the *Mischling* and posed a threat to the purity of the German blood and the innate instinct of the *Volk*. Thus, a race of *Mischlinge*, in between Germanness and Jewishness, was created, which in its structure constitutes a dangerous mixing of the genetic endowments of the German and the Jewish type.[11]

In terms of 'race' and social status '*Mischlinge*' thus were placed between 'Germans' and 'Jews'. Their ostracism included severe obstacles to educational and vocational training and the prohibition to marry outside of their racial category without special permission, which was virtually never granted.[12] At the most extreme, their 'privilege' over 'Jews' spared them from deportation if they 'voluntarily' submitted to sterilisation.[13] By the end of the war, however, the continuing demands of party officials to treat 'first-degree *Mischlinge*' as 'Jews' had led to a severe demise of this 'privileged' status.

Personal narratives represent an important source for the study of '*Mischlinge*' in Nazi Germany, since their treatment was considerably more disparate than the legislation suggests. While some suffered persecution in the same way as 'Jews', a few others received the status of '*Deutschblütige*' and rose within the Nazi hierarchy.[14] In any case, their ambiguous status offered the vast majority opportunities of survival unavailable to 'Jews'. Referring to one parent's 'Aryan' origin sometimes could help conceal the other parent's Jewish descent, and superiors at work and even Nazi officials occasionally eased individual cases of persecution. At the other end of the scale, particularly fanatical officials could extend the persecution of the 'Jews' to '*Mischlinge*', resulting in the deportation of some.[15]

Age and gender contributed further to the significant differences between individual life stories of former '*Mischlinge*'. Due to the fact that their identities had not yet stabilised, children were less capable of resisting the imposed identity and its negative implications. As Oberlaender suggests, children frequently accepted contradicting models of racial, religious and national identities, and their personal narratives indicate conflicting identities from the very beginning.[16] Furthermore, those growing up in the Nazi state faced immense obstacles in areas of personal development, such as education, vocational training and marriage, that could have offered some protection.

Gender-specific differences came into play as a number of male 'first-degree *Mischlinge*' served in the lower ranks of the *Wehrmacht* during the first few months of the war until April 1940.[17] Participating in the war effort nurtured their illusion of having equal status to 'Germans' and some '*Mischlinge*' hoped that as soldiers they could protect themselves and their Jewish relatives from persecution.[18] The marginal involvement of former male '*Mischlinge*' in our survivor project contrasts significantly with the gender division among those interviewees persecuted as 'Jews'. This suggests that the *Wehrmacht* enabled male '*Mischlinge*' to reintegrate themselves temporarily into the 'German' collective, with their potential implication as perpetrators leading them to evaluate their ostracism more ambiguously.

Not only do the biographies of former '*Mischlinge*' differ significantly from each other, but the narrative of Ralf G also demonstrates a scope of agency that explodes the clear-cut dichotomy of perpetrators and passive victims. This dichotomy sustained the thin veneer of post-war German philosemitism, at the cost of silencing more ambiguous accounts of persecution, complicity and survival.

'That didn't faze me': The Biographical Narration of Ralf G

Ralf G was recruited for our project by Gisela M, herself a former '*Mischling*'. Ralf G had only recently begun to speak in public about his Jewish background and his experiences during the Nazi period. Shortly before volunteering for the 'Archive of Memory' he had contributed his story to an exhibition about the Jewish history of his childhood borough.[19] Contacting him proved relatively uncomplicated for the two interviewers of the 'Archive of Memory', and after the separate briefing session his biographical narrative of approximately four hours length was videotaped in one day.[20]

The interviewee's narrative mode appeared composed and jovial, and he gave detailed accounts of his biographical experience without long pauses for thought. In contrast with first-time accounts by other interviewees, Ralf G did not seem to go into deep memory.[21] A comparison between our videotaped interview and a previous tape-recorded question and answer session with students of Ralf G's former school revealed largely fixed narrative structures. At times Ralf G employed identical sentences, used punch lines at the same points of the narration and told the same jokes. Due to the rather problematic content, it may be assumed that the fixed narrative concealed the emotional and ethical conflicts related to Jewish themes and Ralf G's actions during the Nazi period. This impression also emerged from the biographer's frequent response that emotionally charged issues had not really 'fazed' or 'concerned' him ('*das hat mich nicht tangiert*').

The biographer's account of his childhood and youth suggests a highly ambivalent attitude towards Judaism and his family of origin. While the mother remains largely absent from the narrative, Ralf G represents his Jewish father as responsible for his difficult sexual development and personality formation during the Nazi period. Over extended periods of time the interviewee avoided racial ostracism by concealing his Jewish descent, a strategy possibly facilitated by his negative feelings about his father. Franklin Oberlaender observed in the first major study of biographical narratives by former '*Mischlinge*' that those 'who attempted to conceal their Jewish origin had an ambivalent relationship to the Jewish side of the family, to the Jewish parent, or to Judaism'.[22] Commonly, they rejected the more severely persecuted parent of the same sex. Ralf G's narrative indeed suggests a complex interplay between antisemitic and gender stereotypes in his personal identity formation that will be examined here.

For a certain period of time, Ralf G's strategy of concealing his Jewish origin allowed him to circumvent the Nuremberg Laws and to escape social exclusion. However, this strategy had psychological costs despite its apparent short-term gains, as it inevitably entailed the fear of exposure. Although occurring under existential pressure, Oberlaender notes that deception inevitably produces certain complicity with a system of injustice.[23] The implications of such partial acquiescence to Nazi ideology are apparent in Ralf G's largely argumentative and evasive mode of narration. Identifying with certain aspects of the Nazi system provided the interviewee with an apparent solution to the conflicting identities and emotions resulting from his upbringing and the impact of the racial laws yet impeded any lasting sense of belonging.

Childhood and Youth: 'Sure, I was a Jew, but not practising'

Ralf G was born in Berlin in 1919, the son of a Jewish merchant and a non-Jewish telephonist. His recount of the first few years of his life conveys a clearly structured world. Despite his parents' 'mixed marriage', he and his father were members of a Jewish congregation. From 1926 to 1930, he attended a Jewish form in a Catholic community school in Berlin-Schöneberg, receiving instruction both in the Hebrew language and in Christian religion. He regarded himself a Jew, but was too young to notice any differences between Jewish and Christian children. Antisemitic incidents did not occur in his predominantly Jewish environment.

The first distinct rupture of this clearly structured world occurred in 1930, when his parents moved to a working-class neighbourhood with a very small proportion of Jews. As the parents did not 'socialise well' in the new area, the family returned to Schöneberg two years later. The biographer does not elaborate on the causes of their isolation, which may have related to class and ethnic-religious distinctions. A few months after the second move, the father revoked his and his son's membership of the local synagogue 'for the sole reason of saving church tax'. The interviewee, who had been signed up as a baby, describes his reaction to this event as 'completely indifferent':

> Well, a 13-year-old, you see [snorts]. I was a Jew of course, but not practising, I had never been to any church, never to any temple, leaving aside that in primary school the Jewish form went to the synagogue at Münchner Straße on religious holidays. Getting there was ridiculously easy, our schoolyard bordered on the synagogue, so, there was a small door in the fence of the schoolyard that someone would open, and in we went.

Ralf G's postulate that he was 'a Jew of course' sheds doubt on his ostensible indifference toward his disassociation from institutionalised Jewish religion. In fact, argumentation frequently marks a retrospect point of view or justification.[24] The possible contradiction between Ralf G's experience at that time and his narrative construction during the interview also marks his claim that he had not been a practising Jew at all, despite having received Jewish religious education and attending the synagogue adjacent to the school together with his classmates on the relatively numerous Jewish holidays. His narration rejects any agency as he 'neither agreed, nor disagreed' with the father's decision: 'father will know what to do, and it didn't faze me anyway'.

In November 1932, just a few weeks after revoking his Jewish affiliation, the biographer turned 13. Hence his *Bar Mitzvah* was imminent, the rite of symbolically initiating male Jewish youths into the adult community and assigning them responsibility for preserving the religious and cultural heritage of Judaism. The interview does not elucidate whether the father deliberately chose this moment to disassociate from organised Judaism in order to thwart the son's impending *Bar Mitzvah*.

At this point in Ralf G's life a profound immaturity appears to materialise. As he states, he 'developed terribly late' because his father explained the facts of life to him only three years later and at that insufficiently. Although enrolled in yet another school, Ralf G reconnected with his school friends from the Jewish form. But soon he was expelled from their circle because he did not understand their sexual innuendoes:

> It wasn't long before they were telling jokes; naturally, jokes I

> didn't understand as I was a bit on the daft side. Everybody took their turn, one after the other telling a joke, and I could tell great jokes from *Berliner Illustrierte* ... And then, the bombshell dropped, and they were all saying, [falls into Berlin dialect] 'you're no use, we want nothing to do with such a ninny, go home'. And I was really – I lost their friendship because I was such a twit and didn't get their jokes [pauses].

Ralf G's loss of his Jewish friends obviously compounded his uprooting from his Jewish environment that occurred with the family's first move in 1930. Implicitly, however, the biographer blames his father for his expulsion from the group. As he argues elsewhere in the interview, 'sure enough, at one point or another, young people should be introduced to this area', meaning the theme of sexuality. The punitive father not only failed to explain the facts of life to him, but also actively suppressed his sexuality. Every Friday, he checked the son's hands for bitten fingernails – 'somehow this has to do, as doctors found out, with puberty and other such things' – and caned him. These events obviously fuelled the biographer's rejection of his father and of Jewishness, a resentment assuming political significance after the racial laws.

The Nuremberg Laws: 'naïve enough to ... think they contain some kind of gospel'

The Nazis rose to power only three months after the biographer's disassociation from institutionalised Judaism, adding a new dimension to the youth's problematic attitude toward his father and altering his social status. However, Ralf G claims that the new situation was not clearly noticeable until the decline of his father's business after 1935. Furthermore, the father did not detest the National Socialists initially, professing that he would 'rather vote for the National Socialists than the Communists'. Ralf G evaluates his father's response to the election as a 'funny memory', a retrospect rejection of the father for his uncritical attitude towards the Nazis as perhaps accountable for his own *naïve* attitude towards the new regime.

In 1935, however, the Nuremberg Laws took their effect when Ralf G's grammar school closed and his classmates were divided into two groups:

> and now the strange thing happened that all so-called Aryan students went to *Treitschke-Gymnasium* ... and the Jewish students went collectively to *Fichte-Gymnasium*. And I was the only one – I was also the only *Mischling*, though that didn't have anything to do with it – who went to *Goethe-Gymnasium* in Halensee.

The constant rupture of Ralf G's group affiliations, with no close relationships surviving, recurs persistently in his narrative. When transferred to a new form, 'again [composed] half of Jews and half of Christians', Ralf G was forced to revise his family narrative. On demand of his new headmaster the 15-year-old obtained his certificates of descent and found out that his biological mother died shortly after his birth. His father remarried and the second wife adopted the baby. Ralf G professed indifference at this discovery that left his mother 'rather glum ... and maybe even more so because this didn't faze me at all'. Once again, the biographer's insistence that this did not 'faze' him illustrates his response to biographical ruptures by suppressing feelings of sadness or pain.

In 1935 the Nuremberg Laws further challenged the adolescent's increasingly fragile personal reference system. Ralf G's reaction to the term '*Mischling*' elucidates the close connection between the negative connotations of this concept and his stunted sexual development:

> I found this expression funny, but took note of it, and, of course this makes the child coming from a mixed marriage a *Mischling* ... I also know the term *Mischling* from the mix of Dachshunds and Alsatians, of course ... After all, I knew I couldn't marry at all, meeting a *Mischling* girl somewhere would have been purely coincidental. Obviously, where to find one – I wouldn't have known.

Although this statement conveys the biographer's refusal to engage emotionally with the intimate implications of the laws, the animal imagery charges his own intermarried background and sexuality in general with repulsion. However, the 'terribly late developer' was not yet interested in the other sex. Only after his *Wehrmacht* service would he 'have contact with four females altogether' until the close of the war. While his first two girlfriends did not mind his status as a '*Mischling*', both relationships failed because of his 'foolish' behaviour. This obviously refers to his insufficient sexual awareness, as he did not realise 'that women are also interested in doing certain things with men'. Implicitly, he thus again blames his father's failure to explain the facts of life to him for the breakdown of his relationships.

However, it is plausible that both relationships ended also because of the biographer's racial stigmatisation, especially as his first girlfriend's father was an ardent Nazi. On the other hand, it is equally possible that the fear of the legal charge of *Rassenschande* ('race defilement') looming over his first relationship contributed to his sexual passivity. As he states, he complied with his girlfriend's demand and concealed his Jewish origin from her Nazi father because he 'knew what was in store for me – could have been in store for me'.

In another passage of the interview, Ralf G recounts his awareness of his limited marriage options, substantiating the possible link between his sexual inactivity and racial ostracism: 'I read through these things [the Nuremberg Laws] thoroughly and was naïve enough to comply with them, and to think they contain some kind of gospel. Naturally, it didn't cross my mind that this could possibly change later'. This account indicates Ralf G's obvious acceptance of the Nuremberg Laws, which offered him a sense of stability and clear notions of identity in contrast to the unsettling previous years.

Intensifying Persecution of the Jews: 'I did not participate with open eyes'

The 1935 racial laws seemed to make life predictable and enabled the adolescent both to distance himself from the persecuted Jews and to emancipate himself from his father. As the biographer argues:

> on the one hand, the Nuremberg Laws gave you some sense of security, could give you. And you accepted them, but if you gave it a closer look, you could, of course, occasionally notice one thing or another and ask yourself: 'well?!' I for one couldn't have guessed that there would be a Wannsee Conference one day, where *Mischlinge* basically were to be equated with the Jews, such ideas hadn't crossed my mind, weren't mentioned in the law.

While distancing himself from the persecuted Jews eased any sense of severe threat, it presupposed an implicit acceptance of the persecution of the Jews. By 1938, Ralf G seemed to have realised that he could escape social ostracism if he concealed his Jewish origin. The racial laws thwarted his initial plan to become a teacher, so he trained in upholstery after leaving school in 1936. When his training factory became 'Aryanised' two years later, the premature termination of his apprenticeship was imminent. However, he was not asked to prove his 'Aryan' descent and remained the only Jewish employee on the staff.

Ralf G's distancing of himself from the persecution of the Jews emerges clearly in his narration about *Kristallnacht*, of which he claims to have 'virtually no' recollection. In his street, there was 'nothing to be seen at all', but only the Jewish business in the area where he worked 'was demolished, don't know the details, well, didn't go inside, of course, but you could see, was boarded up'. In a lengthy argumentation the biographer explains that at the time he accepted the Nazis' justification for the pogrom as a revenge for the assassination of German diplomat Ernst vom Rath in Paris:

> Of course, this is crazy on the one hand, on the other hand, it is an explanation, after all. Of course, at that time when all sorts of strange things happened, after all, you might as well just believe this, that this is really how it's meant and that later everything will continue normally. What this would really develop into and that a really severe persecution of the Jews would follow you could not necessarily see at that time. You could guess, [falls into Berlin dialect] nothing else [pauses]. And as said before, I'm a matter-of-fact person, and I was, well, it might be true, after all – not only what's happened, what I saw, also what I read in the newspaper of course.

This argumentation functions to justify Ralf G's failure to 'participate with open eyes' in the pogrom, that is, consciously to understand its extent and implications, but it may also indicate retrospect feelings of defensiveness and guilt. Furthermore, this account of the pogrom reveals how Ralf G's seemingly secure position as a '*Mischling*' enabled him ostentatiously to disassociate from the first major physical attack on the German-Jewish population.

Yet his ensuing efforts to circumvent the increasing legal discrimination of '*Mischlinge*' reveal the treacherous nature of the reassurance he paradoxically drew from the racial laws. In mid-1939 he resigned from his position and found a new job, as no one required him to prove his 'Aryan' descent. Changing placements again, he was hired by a former acquaintance who owned a bed feathers factory. In the autumn of 1939 – Germany had just invaded Poland – Ralf G expected to enlist in the *Reich* labour service (RAD), but instead was drafted into the *Wehrmacht*.

'From a normal inner point of view', he states, he would have joined the RAD, yet he thought it

> horrible, being barracked and having to labour, well, this made me feel rather uneasy. Basically I was someone who was his own free person, rather than doing something, er, outdoors – I mean not in the rain, but being on the road, travelling or something along these lines.

Ralf G obviously did not harbour any ideological reservations against Nazi institutions such as the RAD or the *Wehrmacht*, instead creating for himself a normative 'German' biography. His feisty attitude and a good portion of sheer luck helped him to continue to circumvent the racial laws for some time to come.

In the *Wehrmacht*: 'No one assumed that a *Mischling* would be serving there'

Ralf G's narrative of his time in the *Wehrmacht* suggests that he associates military service with adulthood and masculinity, features emphasised in the Nazis' construction of the heroic 'Aryan' soldier.[25] Historically, however, the military had served 'racial' minorities and other socially deprived groups as an integrative force.[26] The *Wehrmacht* provided the biographer with the illusion of having escaped racial ostracism altogether, as no one expected a '*Mischling*' amongst the soldiers. His continued strategy of deception enabled Ralf G to integrate into a group context for the first time since his school days.

Ralf G's interview demonstrates how the military helped him realign the father–son relationship and effected his transition into adult masculinity. Later sexual relationships illustrate how his participation in the German war represented the symbolic initiation into male adulthood that his Jewish father had thwarted. In the biographer's previous representation of the authoritarian and sexually controlling father, the son had implicitly fit the cliché of the emasculate, that is, weak and impotent, Jew promoted by Nazi ideology as the very antithesis of the heroic German soldier. Recounting his time in the military, Ralf G now constructs himself as tall, strong and athletic in contrast to the persecuted father, whom he repeatedly describes with the contemptuous term 'weakling'.

Ralf G's willingness to participate in war action emerges when boredom from staying at the barracks leads him to play – vainly so – in a card game for a placement at the front. In the following, his 'fantastic jackboots', an expression reflecting pride in his uniform, help him hold his own during several consecutive nocturnal 70-kilometre marches following the front on foot: 'We kept on running behind the combat troops, running in the true sense of the word. At that time I was already a bit on the tall side and had to, well, was in the first line'. This highlights the disparity from his father who suffered two hernias during forced labour, as 'a true weakling, looking at me no one would believe that that was my father'. In 1940, however, Ralf G himself had actually suffered from a hernia even before his father, suggesting his own fragile constitution. Because of a shortage of beds in the sick bay, he merely received a truss and the injury healed without hospitalisation. The truss presented by the recovered soldier to his ailing father symbolises the biographer's reversal of the previous power relation between father and son.

Claiming not to have known about the crimes against Jewish and Polish civilians in occupied Poland, Ralf G denies the full implications of his *Wehrmacht* service for the persecution of the Jews. He admits that the Polish civilians were 'not particularly fond of the Germans, but their hatred for the Russians was much greater. The Poles preferred the Germans somewhat over the Russians'. And while discounting the marking of the local Jewish population with blue and white armbands as 'idiotic',[27] he failed to notice any discrimination against the Jews. The Jews were 'running around free, there were no camps', and he even bought 'eggs, by the boxes' from one of them. Typical of German men of his generation, the biographer insists that his job in the orderly room kept him from 'shooting even once, except at the firing range'.

Ralf G thus bridges the gaping chasm between his potential role as a perpetrator and his own racial ostracism. As he argues, his encounters with Polish Jews did not disconcert him, as he was accustomed to 'not telling anyone what's the matter with me'. Hence, he did not experience a severe conflict of identity.[28] It was not necessary for him to deny his Jewish background or conceal his circumcision, simply because nobody suspected the presence of a '*Mischling*'. When asked by the interviewer, he responds with an explanation that he possibly contrives spontaneously. There were, he argues,

> firstly, without a doubt also circumcised people who are not Jews. Secondly, does that really attract that much attention when having a shower [pauses] ... It is rather those who attract attention, I think, who are not circumcised and have an extremely long foreskin, who later on, afterwards, run the risk of getting phimosis and needing an operation, that's what attracts attention.

Ralf G's only account of a personal bond with a fellow soldier illustrates that he did not simply suppress his Jewish past. His companion was a former employee in the leather industry, which like his own trade was considered a 'Jewish' industry before the war. Pride in Ralf G's knowledge of Yiddish shines through when he recounts how both men conversed in the specialist terminology of their professions.

The biographer's apparent identification with his role as a German soldier did not necessarily clash with his Jewish background, since the split between public (German) and private (Jewish) persona represented a central postulate of German-Jewish assimilation. Moreover, his strategy of deception did not directly conflict with the German law. Rather than actively circumventing the latter, he merely withheld information when not questioned directly. In the interview, Ralf G repeatedly stresses his ignorance of the discriminatory legislation, for only after his rise to lance corporal did he learn that '*Mischlinge*' are barred from promotion.[29]

Ralf G's account of his search for the secret decree on discharge for '*Mischlinge*'[30] reveals his enormous fear of exposure and pangs of conscience. Although issued in April 1940, Ralf G did not hear about its existence until a home leave at the end of that year. His search through the filing boxes in his *Wehrmacht* office one night produced the document, yet presented him with a severe conflict: on the one hand, his military service violated German law, on the other hand, he could not simply reveal himself since opening the boxes was equally illegal. Before long, a fellow soldier learnt about the biographer's Jewish origin while on home leave and denounced him. Within days, Ralf G was expelled from service and kept isolated during his final few days in the military.

His comrades 'didn't react at all, all contact immediately ended'. This is the only time that Ralf G's voice betrays the emotional significance of losing yet another context of belonging.

Professional Achievement and Detention: 'It didn't occur to me that they might do me harm'

Ralf G's discharge from the *Wehrmacht* coincided with the commencing deportation of Berlin's Jews and the increasing decline of the 'privileged' situation of the '*Mischlinge*'. The biographer's narration of this period indicates that he continued to deny the intensifying persecution of the Jews and his own impending ostracism, at the cost of minimising the ensuing genocide. In fact, he touches on this theme only when asked, arguing that he had not been aware of the deportations: 'that didn't concern me and my family, after all, my father didn't have to wear the Yellow Badge. Actually, this didn't have anything to do with us'. After all, one of Ralf G's aunts and her family had left for Palestine in 1933, and his father had lost touch with another sister still living in Berlin. 'Friendships with former schoolmates didn't exist anymore' and Jews were absent from his larger environment: 'all the Jewish shopkeepers were gone, the shops had been Aryanised'. Thus, 'nothing [changed], no one knew that I was a *Mischling*'. These passages illustrate how Ralf G's denial of his own precarious situation implied a problematic disregard of the worsening situation of the Jews, an attitude akin to that of many a German bystander.

Instead, the biographer presents a professional success story that contrasts starkly with the perils of emigration, forced labour and deportation that formed the collective experience of the Jews. Agreeing to keep his Jewish descent strictly confidential, he took up his former position at the bed feathers factory and became executive of the company when his employer was drafted into the war. The biographer's 'great contacts' with the German trade authorities let the business prosper and he even received a commission for processing celluloid films for the *Luftwaffe*. The exact circumstances of this job and the content of the films is yet another potentially problematic topic that Ralf G evades. Working for the *Luftwaffe* presumably bolstered his precarious position as it could help explain his status as a civilian. Ralf G's daring insistence on participating in the 'racial' majority represented a form of survival strategy that was aided by unbelievable luck.

However, as with all '*Mischlinge*' and intermarried 'Germans', he was called up for forced labour in 1944 and interned at Zerbst by the *Organisation Todt* (OT).[31] Although rejecting any parallels between his transport from the Grunewald goods depot and the Jews' deportation from the very same station, his argumentation now indicates his awareness of the deadly implications for the latter: 'Jews were taken away, *I* was summoned to the train station, therefore, I had no sense of threat'. This attitude led him to dismiss as an over-reaction the suicide of a fellow deportee during their first night at the camp. He told other labourers to be content with their situation, for as 'Aryans' they would be fighting at the front.

Again, Ralf G's narrative excludes themes such as fear or violence, instead constructing the biographer as an active agent in an adventure story. Being in charge of the food rations granted him permanent permission to leave the camp. Together with the authorities he organised better food for hard labourers and provided nourishing provisions. Travelling to find additional supplies enabled him to visit his parents in Berlin as often as possible. The interviewee's account of how he once caused a stir during a train journey when a sausage hung out of his satchel clearly illustrates the pride in his skills and boldness that he continued to feel.

Ralf G's obvious satisfaction at his privileged situation over fellow camp inmates and the population outside the camp demonstrates the ways in which these 'privileges' helped him to compensate for his racial ostracism. This strategy also marks his argument that the interned '*Mischlinge*' experienced a better lot than German soldiers at the front, an assertion that betrays his disregard for the other inmates. Again, he states his 'extreme luck' as nearly all of his fellow soldiers lost their lives in the war. Through this biographical and narrative strategy the interviewee turns his story of exclusion into one of personal victory and deliverance. It is possible that Ralf G avoids the image of victimisation that is associated with weakness and loss of control also because he wants to live up to traditional male stereotypes in the interaction with his female interviewers.

The Post-War Era: 'Nothing has changed, as it were'

The final days of the war saw the release of the inmates at Zerbst, who were sent to report to the OT in Berlin. Ralf G instead fought his way through southern Germany and is arrested by US Allies near the German–Austrian border. After brief captivity, he returned to West Berlin, married a non-Jewish woman and continued to work in the bedding industry. His father and aunt in Palestine were the only immediate Jewish relatives to survive. Ralf G learnt only after the war that his father's second sister and her son were deported to Riga. Their traces and those of other Jewish relatives remain lost.

Until the mid-1990s Ralf G remained silent about his Jewish background and his ostracism under the Nazis, for there had 'actually been no opportunity, no-one ever asked me about it'. Whenever questioned about the *Wehrmacht* as the collective experience of non-Jewish men of his generation, he referred to his company's strategically important work. In this way, not even his wife's family learnt about his Jewish background. Yet in a debriefing session several weeks after the interview, Ralf G reports in a muted voice that he recently saw a list of his deported classmates. His recent confrontation with the traces of his Jewish past and his willingness to speak publicly about his experiences represent an attempt to approach his story of persecution in all its ambiguities.

In and outside of Germany, engaging with the positionality of '*Mischlinge*' still holds political significance. Those arguing in defence of the perpetrators are all too eager to exploit any ambiguities in the victims' stories and positionalities, asserting that those persecuted were no better than their perpetrators. Writing against this trend, Primo Levi showed how the Nazi system intentionally created shades of 'privilege' and persecution in order morally to implicate its victims and thwart effective resistance.[32] The multifaceted history of '*Mischlinge*' attests to those perfidious gradations of implication and survival, and highlights the complex relationship between Nazi politics and personal agency.

Translated by Matthias Fersterer and Cathy S. Gelbin

NOTES

1. The German original version of this article first appeared under the title 'Zwischen Verfolgung und Anpassung: Die Lebensgeschichte eines ehemaligen "jüdischen Mischlings"', in Cathy Gelbin *et al.* (eds.), *Archiv der Erinnerung Interviews mit Überlebenden der Schoah*, Vol.1: *Videographierte Lebenserzählungen und ihre Interpretationen* (Potsdam: Verlag für Berlin-Brandenburg, 1998), pp.265–98. I thank VBB for the kind permission to reprint the English version of this article, which for technical reasons had to be slightly abridged.
2. Franklin Oberlaender, *Wir aber sind nicht Fisch noch Fleisch: Christliche 'Nichtarier' und ihre Kinder in Deutschland* (Opladen: Leske+Budrich, 1996), p.314.
3. On changing structures of memory in old age, see Eva Lezzi, 'Leben und älter werden in Deutschland', in Gelbin *et al.*, *Archiv der Erinnerung*, pp.357–95.
4. During the 1980s and 1990s, a growing number of studies examined the history of 'mixed marriages' and the children originating from these families during the Nazi period. See, for example, Oberlaender, *Wir aber sind nicht Fisch noch Fleisch*; and Ursula Büttner, *Die Not der Juden teilen: Christlich-jüdische Familien im Dritten Reich* (Hamburg: Hans Christians Verlag, 1988). The increasing interest in the persecution of 'Jewish *Mischlinge*' followed a number of widely received literary and autobiographical publications, such as Ralf Giordano, *Die Bertinis* (Frankfurt am Main: Fischer Taschenbuch Verlag, 1995; also adapted for German television); and Ingeborg Hecht's autobiography, *Als unsichtbare Mauern wuchsen: Eine deutsche Familie unter den Nürnberger Rassegesetzen* (Hamburg: Hoffmann und Campe, 1984). Other literary and personal accounts previously not seen from this angle can be re-evaluated accordingly. See Cathy S. Gelbin, *An Indelible Seal: Race, Hybridity and Identity in Elisabeth Langgässer's Life and Writings* (Essen: Blaue Eule, 2001).
5. See Gabriele Rosenthal's biographical study of family members of the generation of German youth socialised during the Nazi period, *... wenn alles in Scherben fällt: Von Leben und Sinnwelt der Kriegsgeneration* (Opladen: Leske+Budrich, 1987), p.14.
6. Shoshanah Felman and Dori Laub, *Testimony: Crisis of Witnessing in Literature, Psychoanalysis, and History* (New York: Routledge, 1992); and Lawrence Langer, *Holocaust Testimonies: The Ruins of Memory* (New Haven, CT: Yale University Press, 1991).
7. Houston Stewart Chamberlain, *Foundations of the Nineteenth Century* (New York: Howard Fertig, 1977); and Wilhelm Hildebrandt, *Rassenmischung und Krankheit* (Stuttgart: Hippokrates Verlag, 1935), were decisive in developing the supposed link between 'race-mixing' and degeneracy.
8. Robert Weltsch, 'Tragt ihn mit Stolz, den gelben Fleck!', in *Jüdische Rundschau*, 4 April 1933.
9. According to the 1939 census, 72,738 'half-Jews' lived in Germany and Austria, 8,000 of which were 'deemed Jews'. Allegedly, there lived approximately another 30,000 '*Mischlinge*' in the Protectorate of Bohemia and Moravia; see Hans Günter Adler, *Der verwaltete Mensch: Studien zur Deportation der Juden aus Deutschland* (Tübingen: J.C.B. Mohr, 1974), p.281. Based on the percentage of Jews in relation to the non-Jewish German population and the number of 'mixed marriages', the historian Werner Cohn even concludes that some 500,000 Germans were affected by the '*Mischlinge*' category; see Werner Cohn, 'Bearers of a Common Fate? The *Non-Aryan* Christian Fate-Comrades of the Paulus-Bund, 1933–1939', in *LBI Yearbook XXXIII* (1988), pp.327–66, esp. p.350.
10. See the *Reichsbürgergesetz* and the *Gesetz zum Schutze des deutschen Blutes und der deutschen Ehre* (Law for the Protection of German Blood and German Honour) of 15 September 1935, and the two decrees to the *Reichsbürgergesetz* of 14 November

1935, as quoted by Joseph Walk (ed.), *Das Sonderrecht für die Juden im NS-Staat: Eine Sammlung der gesetzlichen Maßnahmen und Richtlinien – Inhalt und Bedeutung* (Heidelberg: C.F. Müller Verlag, 1996), pp.127, 139. This legal position applied to nationals of the German Reich only. In contrast, the category of '*Mischlinge*' did not exist in German-occupied countries such as Poland, where intermarried Jewish and non-Jewish spouses were interned in the ghettos.

11. Wilhelm Stuckart and Hans Globke, *Kommentare zur deutschen Rassegesetzgebung: Reichsbürgergesetz, Blutschutzgesetz, Ehegesundheitsgesetz* (München: Beck, 1936), p.15.
12. The law exempted '*Mischlinge*' from a number of serious anti-Jewish measures, such as being forced to assume the name 'Sara' and 'Israel'. Officially neither companies employing '*Mischlinge*' nor '*Mischlinge*' themselves were to suffer any economic disadvantages. See the decrees of the Reich Ministry of Economics of 25 July 1938 and 3 August 1938, as quoted in Walk (ed.), *Das Sonderrecht für die Juden im NS-Staat*, pp.234, 245. However, as previously mentioned, these 'privileges' were subject to the extremely arbitrary interpretation of individual officials.
13. The debate about the treatment of the '*Mischlinge*' did not lead to a unanimous decision at the Wannsee Conference on 20 January 1942, since some state officials were opposed to subjecting the '*Mischlinge*' to deportation, as, among others, demanded by Reinhard Heydrich. Two further conferences on the Final Solution were dedicated to the question of the '*Mischlinge*', but a decision was reached only in October 1942. The planned sterilisation of 'first-degree *Mischlinge*' was not enforced systematically, as no effective method for mass sterilisation could be developed despite numerous experiments on Jewish and Roma women at Auschwitz and Ravensbrück.
14. The latter group includes, for example, Erhard Milch (1892–1972), Field Marshal General of the *Luftwaffe*, who was Reich Marshal Hermann Göring's protégé. Göring demanded an affidavit from Milch's Jewish mother stating that Milch was his father's extramarital son, that is, not his mother's biological child. See Louis L. Snyder, *Encyclopedia of the Third Reich* (New York: Paragon House, 1989), p.229.
15. See Cathy Gelbin and Angela Reinhard, 'Interview with Irmgard K', as well as Cathy Gelbin and Andrés Nader, 'Interview with Arnold M', Archiv der Erinnerung, Moses Mendelssohn Zentrum Potsdam.
16. See Oberlaender, *Wir aber sind nicht Fisch noch Fleisch*, p.332. However, a Christian-Jewish family *per se* did not necessarily lead to a conflicted identity, but could convey to the child a positive experience of notions of tolerance and cultural-religious diversity. See Cathy Gelbin and Karen Remmler, 'Interview with Gisela M', Archiv der Erinnerung, in which the interviewee recounts her childhood prior to 1935 in a clearly empathic way.
17. See Cathy Gelbin and Vera Stutz-Bischitzky, 'Interview with Ralf G', and Edgar Pankow and Sieglind Schröder, 'Interview with Arno S', Archiv der Erinnerung.
18. See Helmut Krüger's biography, *Der halbe Stern: Leben als 'Mischling' im Dritten Reich* (Berlin: Metropol-Verlag, 1993).
19. 'Formen des Erinnerns: Jüdische und nicht-jüdische Stimmen zur Vertreibung und Vernichtung der jüdischen Nachbarn aus dem Bayerischen Viertel', organised by Kunstamt Schöneberg and the Schöneberg Museum, Haus am Kleistpark, 4 April–2 July 1995.
20. See note 17.
21. For the concept of deep memory, see Langer, *Holocaust Testimonies*, pp.1–38.
22. Oberlaender, *Wir aber sind nicht Fisch noch Fleisch*, p.314.
23. Ibid., p.315.
24. See 'Von den Zeitzeugen zu den Biographen: Methoden der Erhebung und Auswertung lebensgeschichtlicher Interviews', in Berliner Geschichtswerkstatt (ed.),

Alltagskultur, Subjektivität und Geschichte: Zur Theorie und Praxis von Alltagsgeschichte (Münster: Westfälisches Dampfboot, 1994), pp.199–222.

25. Gabriele Rosenthal's biographical interviews with former *Wehrmacht* soldiers demonstrate that interviewees frequently narrated 'their call-up ... as the start of their adult life and manhood, as intended by the Nazi propaganda'. See Rosenthal, ... *wenn alles in Scherben fällt*, p.23.
26. See Oberlaender, *Wir aber sind nicht Fisch noch Fleisch*, p.156. This holds particularly true for the tradition of Jews serving in the Prussian-German army, dating from the early nineteenth century. See Militärgeschichtliches Forschungsamt Potsdam (ed.), *Deutsche Jüdische Frontsoldaten: Von der Epoche der Emanzipation bis zum Zeitalter der Weltkriege*, exhibition catalogue (Hamburg: Militärgeschichtliches Forschungsamt Potsdam, 1996).
27. All Jews from the age of 12 residing in the German-occupied part of Poland had to wear a white armband with a blue Star of David on their right sleeve.
28. In this aspect Ralf G's narrative resembles that of Sally Perel, a Jew according to the racial laws who also served in the *Wehrmacht*. Perel was politically integrated into the Nazi system after being sent to a school of the Hitler Youth movement in Braunschweig. See Sally Perel, *Ich war Hitlerjunge Salomon* (Berlin: Nicolaische Verlagsbuchhandlung Beuermann, 1992).
29. The law barring '*Mischlinge*' from promotion was part of the amendment to the defence act ('Gesetz zur Änderung des Wehrgesetzes'), enacted by Hitler on 26 June 1936, see Walk (ed.), *Das Sonderrecht für die Juden im NS-Staat*, p.166.
30. 'Secret Decree on Discharging *Mischlinge* and the Husbands of Jewesses' (*Geheimerlaß über die Entlassung von Mischlingen und Ehemännern von Jüdinnen*) of 20 March 1940, see Walk (ed.), *Das Sonderrecht für die Juden im NS-Staat*, p.320.
31. In early October 1944, the *Reich* Leader of the SS issued the decree on 'Gathering all Jewish First-Degree *Mischlinge* and Jewish Cross Breeds for Collective Assignment of Labour', see Walk (ed.), *Das Sonderrecht für die Juden im NS-Staat*, p.405. The situation of '*Mischlinge*' and intermarried 'Germans' in the OT's forced-labour camps differed considerably from the situation of Jewish internees in the Nazi concentration camps. There were no selections in OT camps, the food was considerably better and, as Ralf G reports, the internees at Zerbst were addressed by their names rather than numbered. Most survived the internment. The destruction of the death machinery at Auschwitz in late 1944 and the German loss of the war most likely prevented the collective inclusion of '*Mischlinge*' in the annihilation process.
32. Primo Levi, *The Drowned and the Saved*, ed. Erroll McDonald, trans. Raymond Rosenthal (New York: Vintage International, 1989), esp. pp.36–69.

'I wish I could be allowed to choose who I am': Jurek Becker, Victim Identity and Identity Crisis in Post-War Germany

CATHERINE PIGGOTT

Although most commonly regarded as an East German author, Jurek Becker was in fact born in Poland in 1937 and grew up in East Germany after the war. Of Jewish descent, Becker and his family were imprisoned in the Lodz ghetto in 1939. Becker was then transported to Ravensbrück and eventually to Sachsenhausen but later claimed to have no memory of this time. At the age of eight, Becker was reunited with his father, who had survived Auschwitz, and together they moved to Berlin as the only surviving members of the family. Becker, who still only spoke Polish, then faced the considerable challenge of beginning to learn German, and was to acknowledge later in life that part of his motivation for becoming an author was to prove he had finally mastered the German language. After three years studying philosophy at university, his studies cut short by a series of political quarrels with the authorities, Becker began writing, firstly cabaret texts then film scripts, an occupation he followed for most of the 1960s. In 1969 he published his first novel, *Jakob the Liar* [*Jakob der Lügner*], which remains his best-known novel today.

The texts we will examine here are the essay 'Mein Judentum' [My Jewishness], originally written for a radio broadcast in 1977, and the short story 'Die beliebteste Familiengeschichte' [The Most Favoured Family Story], written in the late 1970s after Becker had left the GDR in the wake of the political turmoil surrounding the enforced expatriation of the critical lyricist Wolf Biermann. In addition to so much upheaval in his professional and political life, Becker also separated from his wife during these final months in the GDR. Thus the time at which Becker chose to write these texts, a time when one could reasonably have expected him to continue writing politically critical literature as he had done for most of the decade, is itself indicative of how fundamental the question of his Jewish identity was to him.

Despite the fact that reviewers and literary critics alike had been heralding Becker as a great Jewish author since the publication of *Jakob the Liar* almost a decade earlier, it was not until 1977 that Becker replied to these claims in the text of 'My Jewishness'. Becker opens his essay by calling into question the notion of Jewishness as something one inherits, stating that every time he was asked in the past where he was from he would answer '"My parents were Jews". If the person then went on to say "In that case you are a Jew", I corrected him every time in that I repeated my set phrase: "My parents were Jews". The difference seemed important to me somehow'.[1] The essay goes on to debate Jewishness as a theoretical concept, but as the title suggests, the text reads above all as a very subjective account of how Becker saw his own Jewishness. Becker uses this essay primarily not as a tool for exploring different possibilities or different facets of his identity, as is broadly the case with his 'Jewish' fiction, rather here the message is one of denial, at least initially. Becker acknowledges the consequences his Jewish ancestry had for his own life, not least the fact that, by the end of the war, his vast family, 'previously a great horde of people you could hardly fail to notice, so I have heard, had been reduced to three survivors'.[2] Yet he does not accept that this makes him a Jew. Indeed, Becker refers to the child he was in the concentration camps as 'the person I was at that time',[3] signalling that he sees his post-war identity as something separate to his earlier Jewish social identity, or his family's Jewish roots that caused him to be imprisoned in the first place. This sense of distance from his ancestry is emphasised further by the 'so I have heard', suggesting that this notion of family is something Becker has never experienced directly.

Further to this distinction between his Jewish ancestry and his adult identity, Becker points also to his lack of affinity with the Jewish religion, claiming that he is an atheist. For Becker, choosing to align oneself with a religious group is an intellectual decision and he was angered by others' attempts to pigeonhole him as a Jew: 'I think about this problem so much and become agitated ... because it is decided with irritating frequency by other people who and what I am: amongst other things a Jew'.[4] Yet despite his aversion to others determining his identity for him, Becker was aware of the importance of the perceptions of others when defining one's identity.

> I am well aware that one isn't simply the person one would like to be, rather, like it or not, one also has to be the person others perceive one to be. That is precisely the problem. And seen in this way I have to be the person others judge me to be: a Jew.[5]

Here the reader almost gains the impression that Becker feels he is a victim of his own identity. However, Becker unwittingly undermines his definition of a Jew as someone with a religious or spiritual affinity to Judaism when he defines his father as a Jew, while acknowledging that his father only ever attended the synagogue in order to meet with friends and acquaintances. 'I know that he waited impatiently for the end of the prayers so that he could engage in conversation with the people he had gone there to seek out'.[6] From this one can deduce that although Becker's father had seemingly little religious affinity to Judaism, he was still defined as a Jew by others, not least by his own son.

From early childhood, 'as the only eight-year-old far and wide who couldn't talk properly',[7] Becker was acutely aware of the role played by difference in identity construction and he sought to overcome this difference as quickly as possible by mastering the German language. Similarly, Becker's father felt also that this Jewish identity was largely imposed upon him from the outside as a function of difference. Becker writes: 'Once my father said to me: "If there was no such thing as antisemitism, do you think I would have felt like a Jew for even one second?"'[8] This comment by Becker's father illustrates how he internalised the social identity of Jew that was imposed upon him and thus considered himself to be a Jew. The people he met at the synagogue were not friends from before the war, rather they were people who had also been imprisoned in concentration camps 'and with whom a certain level of natural consensus thus existed'.[9] This affinity only existed as a result of their shared suffering at the hands of antisemites.

For Thomas Jung, 'My Jewishness' reads as a total denial on Becker's part of his Jewish identity, and Jung argues further that Becker did not accept until 1990 that his Jewish ancestry was of any significance to him.[10] We may concur to an extent with Jung, in that Becker continues to deny his Jewishness, especially to critics who would label him a Jew, as he points to his lack of connection to Jewish/family traditions, 'I suspect that traditions mean very little to me anyway', as well as to his atheist convictions to support his case: 'It would have required quite a large effort on my part for me to become a Jew at all'.[11] However, contrary to Jung's claims, there are indications in the essay that Becker goes some way to accepting his Jewishness, even if he is unwilling to admit it. Jung supports his argument by referring to Becker's opening comment that having Jewish parents does not necessarily make him a Jew. Yet these comments are all made in the past tense. '"My parents were Jews". I used this sentence as a stock phrase ... The difference seemed important to me somehow'.[12] This standard answer about his background was something Becker had stopped using already by the time he wrote 'My Jewishness'; rather, Becker had begrudgingly begun to accept the concept of social identity and is even guilty of imposing the identity of Jew on his father, despite the latter's self-proclaimed lack of religious conviction. Finally, Becker concludes his essay with a note of uncertainty.

> I imagine I could be wrong about such an important question ... I don't feel like a Jew, but in a hundred respects I am one. So what? I ask myself to what end am I so intent on solving such a puzzle? Would I be any the wiser? I fear not. I fear I would only try in vain to resolve a secret, without which my life would be poorer.[13]

This conclusion deliberately underplays the significance of Becker's Jewishness and the questions pertaining to it, such as those relating to his family and ancestry, the importance of which Becker initially dismisses. However, he then admits these issues present a 'puzzle' or 'secret' for him, and even confesses he needs this uncertainty, which in itself forms a large part of his identity. Hence Becker's conclusion undermines the earlier sections of the essay in which he denies his Jewish identity; a careful reader of Becker will hardly be taken in by the casual 'I suspect that traditions mean very little to me anyway'.[14] Moreover, Becker's apparent trivialisation of these questions is belied by the frequency and regularity with which he returns to the Jewish thematic in his work. If this argument is valid, then it follows that Becker's denial of the importance of his Jewishness is subverted by the existence of the very text which delivers it.

'The Most Favoured Family Story' is about the art of storytelling itself. The first person narrator retells a story he had heard many times over from his late father about a tradition that had grown out of family gatherings, such events normally taking place to mark the birth of a new child into the family. At these gatherings Uncle Gideon would be called upon to regale the family members with the tale of a fateful business trip he made to London. Gideon completes all his business early 'as you would expect, send Uncle Gideon shopping and he comes back with more money than you sent him with'.[15] He decides to enjoy the rest of his stay in London as a short holiday and is delighted to accept an invitation to a fancy dress party in the place of a business acquaintance who is unable to attend. After much thought Gideon finally decides to go dressed as a clown and spends the better part of a day perfecting his costume, only to arrive at the party and discover not only that he is the sole person in fancy dress, but that he is also the only guest. The business acquaintance has played a cruel, if somewhat unfathomable trick on Gideon. The choice of a clown costume above all others is also no accident, as Jürgen Egyptien shows.[16] With his pointy hat, 'which, in addition to being part of the clown costume, reminds also of the prescribed headwear for Jews in mediaeval Europe', and long coat worn to cover his outfit, 'Gideon has dressed himself similarly to the caftan-wearing eastern Jew'.[17]

It is not so much the story itself as the way in which it is told by Gideon and received by the enraptured audience that is the main content of the text. Before Gideon begins the tale, he must first be coaxed and coerced into it by members of the family/audience, who then urge Gideon on with their laughter, tears, gasps and shrieks as he slowly unravels the story, timing his narrative perfectly to create the maximum amount of tension and thus pleasure for his listeners, who have, in any case, heard this story innumerable times before. As the narrator comments: 'I find the story not bad, but also not particularly meaningful. Its great success must have come from Uncle Gideon's charisma'.[18] The narrator has been told this story at least a dozen times by his father, but never witnessed it himself (apart from at the family gathering arranged to celebrate his own birth). 'It angers me greatly that the ritual we will discuss both started and ended before my time'.[19] Only once in the story is Gideon's fate mentioned: 'Once my father said to me: Gideon was already a very old man by the time they took him to Maidanek, all the same'.[20] This mildly indignant understatement is something of a trademark of Becker's and serves to locate the story historically, as well as offering an explanation as to why this much loved tradition no longer exists.

Critics have almost unanimously focused on the narrative structure of the story as an example of (East European) Jewish family tradition, namely that of oral storytelling.[21] The father attempts to preserve the tradition of the story and the act of telling it as he relates the story 'ten or twenty times' to his son. However, because the narrator/son does not share this urge to retell the story several times, he is attempting to 'write himself free of it' here.[22] Yet before he can write the story down, the narrator has one final problem to overcome. 'The story has several different versions. Every time my father told it, the story was different ... Unfortunately the question has only occurred to me now, and far too late, whether Uncle Gideon could possibly have been the source of the several versions'.[23] The narrator decides to write the story in a manner that encompasses as many elements of the different versions as possible. David Rock points here to the contradictory outcome of the narrator writing the story down, 'thereby giving it a final and enduring shape and so also paradoxically marking both the end of this oral tradition and its perpetuation, since the story will now not be told, but read again and again'.[24]

Contrary to such interpretations, it is not the act of writing down the story that first calls an end to the oral tradition; rather we must concur with the narrator's claim that 'only a force as powerful as Death managed to bring it to an end'.[25] The Holocaust and the destruction of the family meant simultaneously the destruction of the stage on which the story was told (and as the only survivors we learn of are the narrator and his father, who has recently died, there seems to be little chance of new births into the family to revive the traditional gatherings, and indeed little chance of finding enough surviving family members to constitute a gathering). Through the narrator here, Becker expresses his regret at having missed the opportunity to become part of this family tradition, the storytelling is only a small part of this and represents the real tradition, namely the family gatherings at which a new birth into the family is celebrated. For Becker and the narrator, and thus implicitly for other second-generation German Jews, this tradition and sense of family are things they will never experience and which are alien to them. A close analysis of 'My Jewishness' and 'The Most Favoured Family Story' reveals many parallels between the two. In the former, Becker describes his family before the war as 'a great horde of people you could hardly fail to notice, so I have heard'.[26] When the narrator sets the scene in the latter for the great event of the storytelling he talks of the extended family: 'At that time the family was still extensive, I have the phrase *too large to overlook* in mind here'.[27] And later 'According to my father, a sense of family commitment is not just a theory'.[28] In both cases the implication is clearly that the concept of 'family' is something the author and narrator have only heard about from their fathers. The sense of alienation from these roots is further shown by the narrator's reluctance to exchange roles with his father in 'The Most Favoured Family Story', when the father expresses the desire to hear, rather than tell the story. 'I have thought long and hard if I should make the offer for us to exchange roles. I decided not to in the end as it seemed somehow inappropriate to me'.[29] The narrator feels too distanced from this tradition to take a more active role, something that would almost seem like an imposition on his part. This sentiment is echoed by the father, who stubbornly carries out his sense of duty in trying to keep the story alive, but whose nostalgic desire to return to part of the audience of the past suggests also that he finds this story lost in the now diminished family.

When read together, these two texts offer rather a bleak prognosis for second-generation German Jews. Becker's initial vehement denial of other people's insistence of his Jewish identity in 'My Jewishness', and the various arguments he employs in an attempt to achieve this, show that he will remain an outsider in post-war German society as long as he carries this social identity. Moreover, Becker's grudging eventual acceptance of this social identity suggests he sees his status as an outsider as permanent. Indeed, when asked about his Jewishness in the last interview he gave before his death in 1997, Becker replied, 'I wish I could be allowed to choose who I am'.[30]

However, it is not only an externally imposed social identity, but also his own preoccupation with his past and the theme of Jewish family tradition that defines Becker as a Jew here. His casual claim in 'My Jewishness' that 'I suspect that traditions mean very little to me anyway'[31] is contradicted by this clear fascination with tradition in 'The Most Favoured Family Story'. The tradition in question is not so much the story described, but the ritual, regular coming together of the family and the sense of family and community these gatherings afford the members, something for which the narrator yearns. As he is drawn into the sense of familiarity between the members of the audience in the story, with the anticipation that each listener knows how the others will react to certain parts of the story, the narrator admits, almost despite himself, 'that I grew to like Uncle Gideon's story better each time I heard it too'.[32] And here we see the real paradox. While the narrator wishes to become a part of this tradition, the family members are not real people for him, they are simply characters in a story and as such strange and distant. The narrator can only exist outside of, not as a part of this story. This sense of alienation combined with no forum, that is no family gatherings, in which to tell the story, causes the narrator to reject the smaller tradition of oral storytelling, and thus the wider family whose demise he laments, as he finally writes this fluid, fluctuating story down in a solid form.

These two texts represent Becker's attempt at redefining his own identity as a Jew. Whereas he had previously used his writing vehemently to reject a Jewish identity, he has begun to accept the social identity of Jew projected onto him here and we can now detect an almost wistful longing in Becker to embrace his ancestral tradition. Becker would like to feel part of the stories he has heard from his father, yet he has never experienced these events directly and thus cannot find an affinity to this positive Jewish identity. Moreover, the event of the *Shoah* has created a fundamental difference between the generations who witnessed it and remember their suffering and those who do not. Becker's lack of a past that predates the persecution of the Jews prevents him from identifying with the positive image of Jewish culture that the older generation tries to pass on with these stories. The Jewish identity projected onto him by his German compatriots is that of Holocaust victim, an identity which carries purely negative connotations and which is similarly constructed almost entirely as a function of difference to his present surroundings. In the texts discussed here, Becker thus suggests that his crisis of identity is absolute. He has neither memories nor any physical or human reference points to his past, yet this is where factors with which he seeks to construct a positive Jewish identity would lie. Instead, he is defined by social discourse as belonging to a group of (Jewish) victims to whom he feels no affinity. Although Becker suggests in 'My Jewishness' that he is willing to accept this paradox as part of his identity in itself. The desire to resolve this crisis of identity is very much in evidence throughout Becker's work over the next two decades to his death.

NOTES

1. Jurek Becker, 'My Jewishness', in Jurek Becker, *Ende des Grössenwahns* (Frankfurt am Main: Suhrkamp, 1996), pp.9–21, at p.9. All translations from the German are my own.
2. Ibid., p.9.
3. Ibid., p.11.
4. Ibid., p.15.
5. Ibid., p.16.
6. Ibid., p.13.
7. Ibid., p.12.
8. Ibid.
9. Ibid., p.13.
10. Thomas Jung, *'Widerstandskämpfer oder Schriftsteller sein ...': Jurek Becker – Schreiben zwischen Sozialismus und Judentum* (Frankfurt am Main: Peter Lang, 1998), p.13.
11. Becker, *Ende des Grössenwahns*, p.20.
12. Ibid., p.9.
13. Ibid., p.21.
14. Ibid., p.20.
15. Jurek Becker, 'Die beliebteste Familiengeschichte', in Jurek Becker, *Nach der ersten Zukunft* (Frankfurt am Main: Suhrkamp, 1980), pp.40–61, at p.45.
16. For a similar analysis of Becker's choice of costume for Gideon, see Jung, *'Widerstandskämpfer oder Schriftsteller sein ...'*, p.230.
17. Jürgen Egyptien, 'Die Riten des Erzählens und das Stigma der Identität: Anmerkungen zum Verhältnis von Poetologie und Judentum in Erzählungen Jurek Beckers', in Irene Heidelberger-Leonard (ed.), *Jurek Becker* (Frankfurt am Main: Suhrkamp, 1997), pp.279–86, at pp.284–5.
18. Becker, *Nach der ersten Zukunft*, p.42.
19. Ibid., p.40.
20. Ibid., p.42.
21. See, for example, Egyptien, 'Die Riten des Erzählens und das Stigma der Identität'; and David Rock, *Jurek Becker: A Jew who became a German?* (New York and Oxford: Berg, 2000).
22. Becker, *Nach der ersten Zukunft*, p.42.
23. Ibid., p.43.
24. Rock, *Jurek Becker*, p.77.
25. Becker, *Nach der ersten Zukunft*, p.42.
26. Becker, *Ende des Grössenwahns*, p.9.
27. Becker, *Nach der ersten Zukunft*, p.40.
28. Ibid., p.41.
29. Ibid., p.57.
30. Herlinde Koelbl, 'Das ist wie ein Gewitter', *Spiegel*, No.13 (1997), pp.210–16, at p.212.
31. Becker, *Ende des Grössenwahns*, p.20.
32. Becker, *Nach der ersten Zukunft*, p.43.

Inheriting the Holocaust: Transfer of Trauma in Doron Rabinovici's *Suche nach M.*

DENISE DICK

Trans-Generational Transfer of Trauma

The long-term effects of Holocaust traumas on Holocaust survivors were first described in detail by psychiatrist Dr William G. Niederland. In 1968 Niederland published a landmark study on survivor trauma, based on his work with nearly 1,000 Holocaust survivors.[1] He listed in his study a series of traumatic symptoms he had observed in survivors, which he termed 'the survivor syndrome'. Subsequent research would confirm his findings.

It soon became apparent to psychologists that the horrors which survivors had experienced were often too overwhelming to be resolved within the survivors' lifetime. About the same time that Niederland published his findings, other psychologists began documenting symptoms of the survivor syndrome in some children of survivors, or the 'second generation', as they later collectively came to be known, even though they were separated linguistically, culturally, temporally and often geographically from the Holocaust.[2] Psychologists began to theorise that the traumas, which some survivor parents sustained during the Holocaust and from which they continued to suffer, could somehow be passed on to their children. This phenomenon is now frequently referred to in professional literature as 'trans-generational transmission of trauma'.

Strangely, very little research was done on this phenomenon until the late 1970s, roughly a decade after it had first been observed by mental health professionals. Even then, research focused on the *manifestation* of the survivor syndrome in the children of survivors, but rarely was the *process* of transmission from survivor parent to child investigated. Dr Dan Bar-On, Professor of Psychology at Ben-

Gurion University of the Negev, is one of the first to have studied this process. During the 1989–90 academic year, he led a large research project to interview survivor families in Israel. Bar-On suspected that the manner in which children of survivors relate to the Holocaust is influenced by the degree to which their parents have confronted and worked through their Holocaust pasts. Bar-On also theorised that family stories can be both a means of trans-generational transmission of trauma and an indication of how well family members in succeeding generations have worked through this trauma. To test this, he employed a biographical and narrative analysis he and his students developed during a seminar given by Gabriele Rosenthal, at that time Professor for Social Therapy at the University of Kassel.[3] The methodology Rosenthal presented to Bar-On and his students was a technique of biographical reconstruction and analysis which she had used to interview hundreds of Holocaust survivors.[4]

Biographical and narrative analysis starts with a narrative interview with the subject.[5] This interview allows the interviewee to narrate freely without the interviewer guiding or shaping the narration in any way. The narrative choices the interviewee makes during the course of the interview are analysed afterward, with special attention accorded to the differences between the events in the interviewee's life history and how s/he talks about those experiences (his or her life story). According to Rosenthal, it is not coincidental whether an interviewee speaks or remains silent about certain events in his or her life; nor is it mere chance how the interviewee chooses to relate or describe those events to others.[6] Rather, as Dan Bar-On elaborates, the narrative choices (conscious or unconscious) that an interviewee makes allow him or her to skirt events which are still painful; these narrative choices are examples of 'normalization strategies'.[7] This approach, which emphasises a 'narrative truth' (that is, the manner in which someone relates a past event), differs from other methods of narrative analysis which emphasise and pursue a 'historical truth' (that is, the idea that an interviewee's memories can be pieced together to arrive at some approximation of an external, historical reality – what 'really happened').[8]

Bar-On and his research team first determined which events in the survivors' life histories had been included in their life stories, and then analysed which of these events had in turn surfaced in the life stories of their children. They watched closely for the appearance and reappearance of things like particular normalisation strategies and themes in the stories of each generation. Bar-On's research confirms that unresolved traumas from the stories of the survivor parents are being transmitted to their children, chiefly in expressions of fear, suspicion, anger or pain.[9] But his findings were not all negative. He and his team also found instances of what he terms '*spontaneous* processes of transmission and working through' in the families of some survivors.[10] A few families had managed to develop an 'intergenerational healing process' which breaks harmful dialogue and perception patterns, encourages a more open discussion about the past, and limits the transmission of unresolved traumas to future generations.

* * *

Texts by representatives of the second generation are often analysed with the objective of locating the identity of the children of Holocaust survivors.[11] Doron Rabinovici's first novel, *Suche nach M.*, indeed, invites such conceptualisation. This essay, however, by drawing on Rosenthal's and Bar-On's research, attempts an alternative approach by investigating how unresolved Holocaust trauma is transmitted in the fictional Scheinowiz/Fandler survivor family. I have adapted Rosenthal's and Bar-On's research methodology and will first outline the general after-effects and specific traumas evident in the stories and behaviour of Jakob, the survivor parent, and then describe how those themes and issues are taken up in the stories and behaviour of his son, Arieh.[12]

Suche nach M.

Although Doron Rabinovici's parents survived the Holocaust in exile, his novel *Suche nach M.* has several aspects in common with the writings of children of Holocaust survivors. It portrays the complex relationships within two survivor families and the influence of the parents' Holocaust experiences on their children, who were born after the war. It also explores the effect of the parents' silence on themselves and their children. As in some real-life survivor families,[13] the parents in this novel choose silence as a way of protecting their children from the traumas in their pasts. Yet, as Bar-On already has shown, untold stories are just as potent and effective a means of preserving and transferring trauma and unhealed pain as constantly reliving the traumas of the past. This is especially evident in the Scheinowiz/Fandler family. Rabinovici demonstrates the similarities between the lives of Jakob and his son Arieh more forcefully than with the Morgenthau family. For this reason I will draw on the Scheinowiz/Fandler family dynamics in my exploration of the transfer of unresolved trauma from father to son.

Jakob

Although Jakob is a concentration-camp survivor, horrific tales of camp life are conspicuously absent from his life story. This can be explained by the fact that Jakob is extremely reluctant to talk about this part of his life with anyone. Furthermore, Jakob seems to remain more traumatised by what happened to him before his deportation than by the horrors of the concentration camps. These lingering Holocaust after-effects on Jakob present themselves in his post-war life as fossilised survival skills which he adopted first in the ghetto and later in camp: the ability to assume easily a new identity, a strong reluctance to divulge information about himself or his past, and the tendency to flee from (perceived or real) dangerous situations. But these behavioural patterns, which Jakob continues to cling to prevent him from dealing with unpleasant events in his past, adversely affect his relationships with his family and friends.

Jakob's identity has been in flux for so many years that even he seems to have lost track of who he really is. The mainstays of his life began to crumble shortly before the Second World War began. He had two doctoral degrees and taught at the University of Krakau until he was forced to stop teaching because he was Jewish. His wife Hannah left him for another man, taking his young daughter with her; both would perish later in the Holocaust. Shortly thereafter Jakob went into hiding under the assumed name of Jakob Fandler.

But his identity problems do not end there. Jakob survived a raid on the ghetto in Krakau because he was mistaken for the printer Adam Kruzki, whom the Nazis wanted to keep alive for a while longer to use his expertise. Because this incident of mistaken identity postponed his deportation, it quite possibly allowed him to survive the camps. But it also haunted him for years to come, in part because

Jakob is convinced that Kruzki died in his place. Being mistaken for Kruzki years after the war by an old man who is a patron of Jakob's favourite café only exacerbates his feelings of guilt. Each time they meet, the old man would tell Jakob that he should never have sold his printing business. Initially Jakob denies each time that he was the printer Kruzki, but after a while he resigns himself to admitting that the old man was right.

When Jakob meets Tonja Kruzki during a Rosh Hashanah celebration at his friend's house, he takes cruel and spiteful advantage of his resemblance to Adam Kruzki. Jakob predicates his own identity on the identity and the desires of his conversation partner ('*Tonja, ich bin's, wenn du's bist*'),[14] and although he never does fully understand why he sustains his masquerade as Tonja's former husband, he exploits the situation fully. Both Tonja and Jakob have unresolved issues with their former spouses (both of whom did perish in the Holocaust), which this encounter allows them to address. It is a cathartic 'reunion' which gives both a sense of closure, however brief and illusory. The circumstances of the collapse of their respective relationships were similar enough that Jakob can convincingly bluff his way through the conversation, posing as Adam while asking Tonja the questions he never had the opportunity to ask his wife, Hannah. In this way Jakob is able to reproach his former wife (with Tonja as her stand-in) without ever actually confronting his painful past.

Jakob flatly rejects Tonja's suggestion that they could build a new relationship now that they are both single again. Tonja concedes that it would be pointless; after all, she subtly reproaches him, he has not changed a bit (p.18). Years later, when telling his friend Leon Fischer about the awkward encounter with Adam Kruzki's widow, Jakob recalls feeling '*daß keine Rückkehr möglich wäre, selbst wenn sie Hannah oder ich Adam wäre, wir könnten nie mehr zusammenkommen*' (p.99). There is no turning back either in another sense: Jakob can no longer bring himself to reveal his true identity to Tonja. He quickly ducks out of the dinner party, only to bump into the old man from his favourite café outside. Jakob is once again reminded of his Adam Kruzki identity, and the old man excitedly reports that he has seen Jakob's 'wife' Tonja earlier that day. This proves too much for Jakob, who grabs the old man and flies into a confessional rage, admitting to occasionally taking advantage of his resemblance to Kruzki, but now identifying himself, significantly enough, by his former occupations. The old man manages to pull free from Jakob's grip and sputters back: '*Glauben Sie, ich weiß nicht, wer Sie waren? Ich weiß genau, wer Sie waren – aber wer auch immer Sie waren, Sie sind es nicht mehr*' (p.23).

Tonja's and the old man's observations about Jakob are not as contradictory as they might initially seem to be. Paradoxically, Jakob is no longer who he once was, yet he has not changed. For years his response to a threatening or dangerous situation has been to hide behind false identities. This was an immensely useful survival skill during the war, but it brings him no peace thereafter. Jakob feels he is living on borrowed time bought with Adam Kruzki's life, and he cannot forgive himself for leading Kruzki's widow to believe that her husband rejected her at their chance meeting at the Fischers' flat.

After his painful encounter with Tonja, Jakob once again creates a new identity behind which to hide, this time attempting to distance himself from his painful past. He switches his name back to Fandler, the assumed name he lived under while in hiding, he marries a Jewish woman half his age, he withdraws from the Jewish community, and he moves without notifying any of his friends. Jakob simply abandons his old life, discarding it for a new life and a new identity. So complete is the break with his past that 20 years later, when at last reunited with his friend Leon Fischer, Jakob would tell him, '*Scheinowiz ist nicht mehr, ich habe ihn sterben lassen*' (p.97).

Jakob's marriage may also have provided him with a refuge from his horrific past. His wife Ruth was just a young girl when war broke out, and her family survived in exile, returning to Europe some years after the war. It is not unusual for a survivor to identify more strongly with a non-survivor spouse's background and family as a way of separating from his or her own painful past.[15] Indeed, his marriage to Ruth marks the beginning of his exile from his old life and from his circle of survivor friends. It is also conceivable that Ruth, not wanting to upset her husband, would not have pressed him to talk about that period of his life. What emerges from the text, however, is that Jakob finds their lack of shared experience isolating. The completely different circumstances under which Jakob and his young wife each survived the Holocaust lead him to assume that she could never understand what he had endured. His steadfast refusal to confide in Ruth isolates him further still.

Arieh

There is a different explanation for Jakob's emotional isolation from his son, Arieh. Jakob tries to keep his former life from his son in a desperate attempt to protect Arieh from the unresolved traumas of his father's past. So secretive is he about his past that even when Arieh says he knows almost nothing about Jakob, his father answers cagily, '*Wer ich war, wird auf meinem Grabstein stehen. Ein wenig Geduld, mein Sohn*' (p.49).

However, Jakob's old traumas, lingering guilt and his general view of the world still shape his relationship with his son from the moment Arieh is born. Jakob and Ruth decide to give their son two first names, one Christian and one Jewish, so that he will be accepted in both communities – and more importantly, so that he will be able to choose between the two, thereby enabling him to sidestep potential persecution (p.139). Arieh's double name (Arieh Arthur) also recalls the double life that his father (first as Jakov Scheinowiz, then as Jakob Fandler) has led for so long.

Because Jakob was beaten in the camps, he expects Arieh to be able to defend himself physically, so he enrols his son in martial arts classes. But Arieh eschews both physical contact and direct confrontation, preferring an indirect, intellectual approach to life's problems. He excels in mathematics and delights in solving complicated equations with multiple variables, which is fortunate as his life is littered with unknowns, and his father is a puzzle that he has not yet been able to solve.

Unfortunately, knowing that certain topics are not open for discussion in his family does not protect Arieh from them; it only piques his curiosity, and he is soon seeking answers elsewhere. Arieh grows up with the children of his mother's Jewish school friends, and it is through them that he hears about the Jewish student organisation. Much to his father's displeasure, he begins to build contacts with its members, '*um zu finden, was zu Hause ihm vorenthalten worden war, um jene Chiffren und Kennworte des Codes zu erlernen, in dessen Geheimnis er daheim nicht eingeweiht wurde*' (p.45). It is made very clear that Arieh associates with the club only to satisfy his own curiosity about his family background: he does not work for the organisation, '*sondern an sich selbst – mit Hilfe der anderen jüdischen Jugendlichen*' (p.45).

It must be stated here that the preternatural over-sensitivity to others' culpability that Arieh develops as he matures grows from a combination of his awareness of his father's unresolved guilt, his ignorance of his family history and lack of personal identity, and his inclination to search for answers outside of himself and his family. This aspect of Arieh's personality goes beyond a realistically plausible description of the second generation and into the uncannily fantastic. Here Rabinovici exaggerates an aspect of Holocaust after-effects in the second generation to build suspense in *Suche nach M.* and to raise and address issues of guilt, responsibility and the social identity of minorities in Austrian society, issues which are not pertinent to this discussion. It is significant, however, that Rabinovici makes use of trans-generational transfer of trauma to explore these wider issues. Furthermore, Rabinovici continues to show the after-effects of Jakob's unresolved traumas on his son and Arieh's struggle to come to terms with these after-effects through to the conclusion of the novel.

As he grows older, Arieh becomes more adept at impersonating and tracking down those who attempt to conceal their guilt. His decision to stalk Herwig Wernherr, the leader of a neo-Nazi group which attacked Jewish youths in a local club, can be misinterpreted as an indication that Arieh now identifies himself as a Jew. But the text reveals that this hunt for the guilty differs fundamentally from Arieh's previous ones. He now seeks someone who has not wronged him personally, and Arieh hopes that by tracking down the perpetrator he will be able to understand himself better.

The resulting shift to the extreme right in Arieh's taste in clothing, hairstyle and reading material eventually forces a confrontation with his father. It could have been an opportunity for some honest sharing, but Jakob is unable to bridge the years of silence in one evening. He sketches his past to his son in only the barest details, and when he tells Arieh of his assumed name and real identity, Arieh asks his father whom that makes him. His father can only offer the limp advice: '*Das ist deine Sache. Das mußt du selbst entscheiden*' (p.58). Instead of redirecting Arieh to look for answers to his own identity within himself, Jakob's hands-off approach strengthens Arieh's resolve to seek it in others. Arieh suddenly realises that he '*mu[ß] sich beim Feind unter falschem Namen und als Freund einschleichen, denn er, Arieh, war ein anderer, würde nie zu sich finden, solange Wernherr nicht bezwungen war*' (p.59). This course of action marks a notable difference between father and son: while Jakob pretends to be someone he is not to protect himself and his family from who he really is, Arieh searches for clues to his identity among those who he is *not*.

Arieh's process of elimination, as it were, goes terribly wrong. He inadvertently kills Herwig Wernherr and is forced to flee Austria. Ironically, his panicked flight to Israel drives Arieh into the arms of Jakob's past, although it is not Arieh's choice of destination so much as his chosen course of action (running away from what he cannot bear to face) that mirrors previous events from his father's life. He is no longer an uncertain Jew living in the Diaspora, but an irresolute Jew reluctantly living in Israel, whose over-sensitivity to the guilt of others is pressed into service by the Israeli Secret Service to track down spies and other enemies of the State of Israel. He is forced further and further into roles and situations which define his identity in extremes without leading him to a better self-understanding. His hope of finding peace and gaining some self-insight is thwarted when he finds himself trapped in a deal that forces him to make a living assuming the identities of others to protect himself.

Arieh seems doomed to imitate his father's coping skills. He too adopts new identities with amazing ease, a skill which proves indispensable to him as an Israeli Secret Service agent, but leaves him only more confused about his real identity. Indeed, his ability to take on the identity of others has overwhelmed his own identity; his entire life centres on flushing out enemies of the State of Israel for his Secret Service colleagues. This is a twist on an aspect of his father's history. While Jakob castigates himself for a death for which he was not responsible, Arieh tracks down targets for his colleagues to kill, but he cannot face his own responsibility in these murders (p.110f.).

We soon see other patterns from Jakob's life re-emerge in Arieh's, with some slight variations. Arieh, like his father, marries a woman from 'outside' his background and culture and even takes her name, Bein. Navah is an Israeli of German descent whose command of German is that of a foreign language. Navah is more interested in Arieh's past and professional activities than Ruth seemed to have been in Jakob's, but Arieh's long absences and his steadfast refusal to open up to her dampens her attempts to communicate with him. A silence similar to that in the Fandler household subsequently settles in among the Bein family members too. Of course, the top-secret nature of his work prevents Arieh from discussing his job with his wife, but his long absences from home also play a role in their increasing estrangement from each other. Initially, Navah complains to Arieh about his absences from the family, but after a while she immerses herself in her research, and withdraws to her study on the few occasions when Arieh is around to take care of their daughter, Jael.

Navah seems more perceptive of Arieh's inner struggles than Ruth was of Jakob's, and she does not hesitate to address them. Shortly after his first encounter with Mullemann in the hospital, Arieh takes an extended leave of absence, ostensibly pleading exhaustion. The encounter has left him deeply troubled, but he has never learned how to confide in anyone close to him. Fortunately, Navah is able to pinpoint the source of his exhaustion and voices her concern for him: '*Deine Erschöpfung, Arieh, rührt von deiner Unruhe, dieser Suche nach anderen, mit der du dir ausweichst*' (p.145). But Navah's identifying what troubles Arieh does not free him from it. He continues to avoid both himself and those closest to him, especially his daughter. Again, Navah is the one who sees the pattern of revisited and relived trauma that is unfolding in their family, and it falls to her to confront her husband with it:

> *Arieh, du wiederholst an deinem Kind alles, was dein Vater dir antat. Begreifst du nicht? Du bist nur ein Gast für uns. Sie weiß nicht, wer du bist! ... Du bist wie Jakov Scheinowiz, dein Vater, als lebtest du im Untergrund, versteckst dich vor der Vernichtung. Auf ewiger Flucht. Unter falschem Namen* (p.152f.).

Rabinovici strengthens the link between the identity crises of father and son with a dream they both have about paying for a new identity in a café. Both the dream and the life circumstances in which Jakob and Arieh have the dream are strikingly similar. It comes to them when their guard is down: Jakob is in a fragile mental state and awakens from his dream to find himself in hospital; Arieh is relaxing on the beach while on assignment. Both have the dream during a personal crisis, too: Jakob had just been notified of his mother's death and learned of his son's emigration to Israel; Arieh has discovered that his wife has been sleeping with a rival colleague. Both father and son have the dream when they have either been given or have assumed another person's identity: Jakob was mistakenly admitted to the hospital under the name Adam Kruzki because he was babbling the name before he collapsed; Arieh is on assignment, working under an assumed name.

Their dreams do differ in two significant aspects, however. First, Jakob's dream – in contrast to the rest of the novel – is narrated in the first person, and the style of narration manages to convey simultaneously deep personal revelation and self-estrangement. The dreamer refers to himself twice as '*der ich bin*' before slipping into the customary first-person form of self-reference, '*ich*' (p.88f.), which makes it difficult to think of the dreamer and Jakob as one and the same person. Arieh's dream lacks the lucid immediacy of his father's because it is narrated in the third person and in the past tense. Furthermore, the resemblance of Arieh's dream to his father's creates the impression that Arieh is not dreaming his own dream but instead that his father's dream has come to haunt him. The second notable difference is the conclusion of their dreams, which reflect their personal lives. Jakob pays too much (with money in his dream, in personal sacrifice in real life) for a new identity, and he awakens saying who he *is*. Arieh, however, dreams he has taken on the identity of someone whom he is to kill, just as he is required to do in real life. He awakens saying who he is *not*. It is instructive to recall that up until this point Arieh had chased after people he did not know personally in an effort to discover who he himself really is.

The remainder of the novel focuses largely on Arieh's dealings with Mullemann who, underneath all the bandages, is really his childhood friend Dani. Dani's loss of his own identity and assumption of the guilt of others trigger deep personal changes in Arieh. Once back in Israel, Arieh describes some of these changes in a letter to Dani. He writes that he has given up his job with the Israeli Secret Service so he will no longer be chasing after the guilty and the enemies of the state in order to arrange for their murders. The First Gulf War has changed his life, too. Arieh writes to Dani about the precautions they have taken against a biological or poisonous gas attack, and what it feels like to be under the constant threat of such an attack: '*Es raubt uns den Atem, obwohl noch keine Giftschwaden über uns versprüht wurden. Die Vergangenheit qualmt aus den Ritzen*' (p.249). A sudden attack provides an alarming but ironic confrontation with the past right in Arieh's own home. The sirens sound, and Arieh gathers his family in the sealed room in their apartment.

> *Ruth streifte Jael die Maske über, die eigens für Kleinkinder angefertigt worden war, dann setzten sie die Gummilarven auf ... Sie verwandelten sich in Ameisen oder Kakerlaken mit Filterrüsseln und riesigen Glasaugen. Sie wurden Insekten, die sich kaum noch bewegten und angestrengt atmeten* (p.249).

In Hitler's Germany, propaganda figuratively reduced the Jews to vermin, which had to be exterminated. But in modern-day Israel, Arieh and his family temporarily metamorphose into insects in order to survive.

After the early morning attack, the family returns to bed and Arieh continues his letter to Dani. He writes that he has decided to look for himself by looking into himself and by learning about his past. After the war is over, he plans to travel to Krakau with Leon Fischer, his father's close friend, to learn about his father's past. This change in Arieh's attitude is promising; it is a modest example of what Bar-On has referred to as a spontaneous instance of working through the past. Jakob has been dead for years at this point, so Arieh can no longer hope to open a healing dialogue with his father. But perhaps through extensive introspection and learning as much as he can about his father's life history, Arieh can liberate himself from some of the influences of his father's past and counteract their effects on him before they too deeply affect his daughter.

Suche nach M. is often viewed as an exploration of post-war Jewish identities. Clearly the second-generation character Arieh wrestles with his identity in post-war Austria and Israel. Fundamental to his struggle is his father's legacy of guilt and unresolved traumas, issues that transcend that of religious identification or affiliation. The research of Gabriele Rosenthal and Dan Bar-On has expanded our awareness of the influence of survivor parents' unresolved traumas on the lives of their children and grandchildren. It also deepens our understanding of this additional factor in the second generation's struggle to develop identities in post-Holocaust society, especially as this struggle is portrayed in the literature of the second generation. Rosenthal's and Bar-On's findings augment the analysis of Arieh's struggles with his sense of self and his roles in his family and post-Holocaust society.

NOTES

1. William Niederland, *Folgen der Verfolgung: Das Überlebenden-Syndrom. Seelenmord* (Frankfurt am Main: Suhrkamp, 1980).
2. For an overview of the issues the second generation faces as described in professional psychological literature, see Martin S. Bergmann and Milton E. Jucovy (eds.), *Generations of the Holocaust* (New York: Columbia University Press, 1982); and Aaron Hass, *In the Shadow of the Holocaust: The Second Generation* (Ithaca, NY: Cornell University Press, 1990; Cambridge: Cambridge University Press, 1996). For an account directly from the perspective of a child of Holocaust survivors, see Helen Epstein, *Children of the Holocaust: Conversations with Sons and Daughters of Survivors* (New York: Putnam, 1979).
3. Dan Bar-On, *Fear and Hope* (Cambridge, MA: Harvard University Press, 1995), pp.12, 353.
4. For an outline of Rosenthal's methodology and her conclusions, see Gabriele Rosenthal, *Erlebte und Erzählte Lebensgeschichte: Gestalt und Struktur biographischer Selbstbeschreibungen* (Frankfurt am Main: Campus, 1995); and Gabriele Rosenthal (ed.), *The Holocaust in Three Generations: Families of Victims and Perpetrators of the Nazi Regime* (London: Cassell, 1998).
5. Rosenthal prefers the term 'biographical' to 'autobiographical' in this context because 'the latter term does not place adequate emphasis on the social construction of life stories'. See Gabriele Rosenthal, 'Questions and Method', in Rosenthal (ed.), *The Holocaust in Three Generations*, p.6, n.5.
6. Ibid., pp.4–5.
7. Bar-On, *Fear and Hope*, pp.34–5.
8. Ibid.
9. Ibid., p.332.
10. Ibid., p.333 (original emphasis).
11. For a discussion of the issues of post-Holocaust Jewish identity, see Lynn Rapaport, *Jews in Germany after the Holocaust: Memory, Identity and Jewish–German Relations* (Cambridge: Cambridge University Press, 1997).
12. For a similar analysis of three other fictional works by second-generation authors in light of Rosenthal and Bar-On's findings, see Denise Dick, 'After-Effects of the Holocaust as Expressed in German Literature', Ph.D. dissertation, Wayne State University, 2004.
13. See, for example, Epstein, *Children of the Holocaust*.
14. Doron Rabinovici, *Suche nach M.* (Frankfurt am Main: Suhrkamp Taschenbuch Verlag, 1999), p.17 (all further page references to this volume are in the main text); published in English as *The Search for M* (Riverside, CA: Ariadne Press, 2000).
15. The case study of the Stern family is just one example of a survivor spouse seeking refuge in a marriage with a non-survivor. See Waltraud Schade, Sabrina Böhmer and Gabriele Rosenthal, 'Shared and Divided Worlds: The Stern Family', in Rosenthal (ed.), *The Holocaust in Three Generations*, pp.95–117.

Abstracts

Children's Voices and Viewpoints in Holocaust Literature
SUE VICE

In this essay I will discuss some examples of Holocaust writing by, or about, Jewish children during the Holocaust years. These two categories consist respectively of contemporary material written by children, including diaries and testimony or memoirs by adult survivors looking back at their childhood selves; and fiction. In the latter, literary and narrative techniques used to convey children's experience are very varied and are often designed to present what is distinctive about a child's viewpoint. Both kinds of text, contemporary and retrospective, may include such elements as misunderstanding, gaps in memory and varieties of irony, but, I will argue, do not – and indeed cannot – include any representation or sample of a child's own language or voice.

Drawing the Holocaust in 1945
NICHOLAS STARGARDT

In the early summer of 1945, the Swiss Red Cross invited 300 child survivors of the camps to recuperate in Switzerland for a few months. Many of the children came from Buchenwald. Among them were two Jewish boys of 16: Kalman Landau was Polish, Thomas Geve, German. Both had survived Auschwitz, Buchenwald and the evacuation marches to Groß-Rosen in the snows of January 1945, and – at different times – both drew pictures to illustrate their experiences. A cycle of Landau's 12 pictures would be published in the Swiss magazine *Du* in March 1946; Geve's had to wait another 50 years, mainly for family reasons, before Yad Vashem and the Gedenkstätte Buchenwald brought them into public view. This essay explores the ways in which these teenage boys expressed their experience of the Holocaust in art during the first months after their liberation.

Stolen Childhood: Austrian Romany Ceija Stojka and her Past
SUSAN TEBBUTT

In her moving autobiographical accounts *Wir leben im Verborgenen* (1988) and *Reisende auf dieser Welt* (1992) and in the poetry volume *Meine Wahl zu schreiben* (2003), which includes images of some of her paintings, Austrian Lovara Romany Holocaust survivor Ceija Stojka creates a unique account of the pain and trauma of her childhood under the Nazis. Whilst presenting dystopian images of the suffering of her family she never becomes bitter, and offers substantial insights into the world of the Romanies. In so doing she reclaims in part her stolen childhood and highlights the importance of all children, whatever their racial origins.

Between Adult Narrator and Narrated Child: Autobiographical Writing by Former Members of the *Kindertransporte*
ANDREA HAMMEL

This essay uses several autobiographical texts by former members of the *Kindertransporte* to discuss the tension between institutional history and personal life stories in relation to a number of issues present in these texts. Authenticity, group identity, the cultural construct of the 'child' concept and the fragmented self are examined within the framework of Holocaust memoir writing and cultural and autobiographical theory. The essay argues for a multidimensional analysis of such autobiographical texts to reach a wider audience within and outside Holocaust studies.

Between Persecution and Complicity: The Life Story of a Former 'Jewish *Mischling*'
CATHY S. GELBIN

The particular treatment of persons of 'mixed' Jewish and non-Jewish ancestry during the Holocaust remains an under-explored topic in scholarly research on the Holocaust. Drawing on the relatively new field of biography studies in Germany, this essay looks at the life history of a former 'Jewish *Mischling*' in Germany to exemplify the ways in which circumstances such as age, gender and religious affiliation affected the diverse treatment of individuals belonging to this persecuted group. Ralf G's personal narrative is contextualised within the Nazi debate on the definition and treatment of 'mixed-race Jews' to show how these discourses and political practices impacted on the individual self-construction of persons from intermarried backgrounds at the time of persecution and into the post-war period.

'I wish I could be allowed to choose who I am': Jurek Becker, Victim Identity and Identity Crisis in Post-War Germany
CATHERINE PIGGOTT

This essay examines two texts by Jurek Becker (1937–97), who spent his early years in Ravensbrück and Sachsenhausen, later claiming to have no memory of this. Becker's essay 'My Jewishness' reads as a vehement denial of his Jewish identity, which in a post-war German context is synonymous with victim. Becker seeks to disassociate himself from his past and subvert this unwanted social identity. Nevertheless, Becker is still intrigued by his past and mourns the death of his family in 'My Favourite Family Story', where the Jewish narrator laments the loss of great family traditions, which he has often heard about but never experienced. This essay suggests that together these two texts show that, for Becker, children of the Holocaust carried the identity of outsiders in post-war Germany. Defined and stigmatised by contemporary society as a victim and 'other', Becker could not access this past that continued to construct his social identity. His family and its traditions are reduced to characters in a story for Becker; he is caught in the tension between past and present, at home in neither.

Inheriting the Holocaust: Transfer of Trauma in Doron Rabinovici's *Suche nach M.*
DENISE DICK

Psychologists have observed that unresolved Holocaust traumas can be passed from survivors to their children. This phenomenon, termed trans-generational transfer of trauma, is also evident in some literary works of second-generation authors. This essay provides a brief introduction to the theory of trans-generational transfer of trauma and shows how it can provide another way of reading the literature of second-generation authors, such as Doron Rabinovici's first novel, *Suche nach M.* (1999).

Notes on Contributors

Andrea Reiter, Senior Lecturer in Modern Languages and Parkes Fellow at the University of Southampton, is the author of *Narrating the Holocaust* (2000) and has published on contemporary Austrian literature. She is currently completing a book on the German exile writer Hans Sahl.

Sue Vice is Professor of English Literature at the University of Sheffield. Her most recent book is *Children Writing the Holocaust* (2004).

Nicholas Stargardt is a fellow in modern European history at Magdalen College, Oxford. He has written *The German Idea of Militarism: Radical and Socialist Critics, 1866–1914* (1994) and *Witnesses of War: Children's Lives under the Nazis* (2005).

Susan Tebbutt, Head of German Studies at Mary Immaculate College, University of Limerick, is the co-editor with Nicholas Saul of *The Role of the Romanies* (2004) and editor of *Sinti and Roma: Gypsies in German-Speaking Society and Literature* (1998). She is currently completing a cultural history of Romanies and genocide.

Andrea Hammel is AHRC Research Fellow and Project Coordinator at the Centre for German-Jewish Studies at the University of Sussex. On the *Kindertransport* subject she has co-edited *Kindertransporte 1938/39: Rescue and Integration*, special issue of *Shofar* (2004) and her monograph on *Everyday Life as Alternative Space in Exile Writing* is forthcoming in 2005.

Cathy S. Gelbin (Ph.D., Cornell University) is currently based in the Department of German Studies at the University of Manchester. Her research and teaching focus on constructions of Jews and gender in nineteenth- and twentieth-century German culture. Select publications include *An Indelible Seal: Race, Hybridity and Identity in Elisabeth Langgässer's Writings* (2001), *AufBrüche: Kulturelle*

Produktionen von Migrantinnen, Schwarzen und jüdischen Frauen in Deutschland (co-ed., 1999), and *Archiv der Erinnerung: Interviews mit Überlebenden der Shoah. Videographierte Lebenserzählungen und ihre Interpretationen* (co-ed., 1998).

Catherine Piggott completed a Ph.D. on themes of identity in the works of Jurek Becker at the University of Bath before becoming a secondary school teacher of German and French.

Denise Dick earned her doctorate from Wayne State University; she wrote her dissertation on the literature of the children of Holocaust survivors. She lives in Redmond, Washington, with her husband.

Index

Page references to non-textual information such as drawings are in *italic* print